Jesus is Not Safe

Jesus is Not Safe

WANG BIN YU

CASCADE *Books* · Eugene, Oregon

JESUS IS NOT SAFE

Cascade Books
An Imprint of Wipf and Stock Publishers
199 W. 8th Ave., Suite 3
Eugene, OR 97401

www.wipfandstock.com

PAPERBACK ISBN: 978-1-5326-3961-6
HARDCOVER ISBN: 978-1-5326-3962-3
EBOOK ISBN: 978-1-5326-3963-0

Cataloguing-in-Publication data:

Names: Yu, Wang Bin, author.

Title: Jesus is not safe / Wang Bin Yu.

Description: Eugene, OR: Cascade Books, 2018 | Includes bibliographical references.

Identifiers: ISBN 978-1-5326-3961-6 (paperback) | ISBN 978-1-5326-3962-3 (hardcover) | ISBN 978-1-5326-3963-0 (ebook)

Subjects: LCSH: Jesus Christ—Person and offices. | Jesus Christ—Teachings.

Classification: BT202 .Y70 2018 (print) | BT202 (ebook)

Manufactured in the U.S.A.   OCTOBER 26, 2018

To David Hawkins
whose faith is known to God

Contents

.

Introduction

The Lion, the Witch, and the Wardrobe is a book that everyone should read. It is an allegory about Christian faith: the "lion" (whose name is Aslan) is Jesus; the "witch" is the devil; and the "wardrobe" is the kingdom of heaven. Close to the beginning of this little book, Susan and Lucy have a telling conversation with Mr. and Mrs. Beaver:

> "But shall we see him?" asked Susan. "Why, Daughter of Eve, that's what I brought you here for. I'm to lead you where you shall meet him," said Mr. Beaver. "Is—is he a man?" asked Lucy. "Aslan a man!" said Mr. Beaver sternly. "Certainly not. I tell you he is the King of the wood and the son of the great Emperor-beyond-the-Sea. Don't you know who is the King of Beasts? Aslan is a lion—the Lion, the great Lion." "Ooh!" said Susan, "I'd thought he was a man. Is he—quite safe? I shall feel rather nervous about meeting a lion." "That you will, dearie, and no mistake," said Mrs. Beaver; "if there's anyone who can appear before Aslan without their knees knocking, they're either braver than most or else just silly." "Then he isn't safe?" said Lucy. "Safe?" said Mr. Beaver; "don't you hear what Mrs. Beaver tells you? Who said anything about safe? 'Course he isn't safe. But he's good. He's the King, I tell you."

Jesus is good, but he is not safe. All who have Christian faith believe that Jesus is good: Jesus is good because in him we understand and experience the goodness of God—but few Christians believe that Jesus is not safe. Jesus is not safe because he calls us to turn from everything in the world that is between us and God: we are to repay curses with blessings and violence with love; we are to give our money to the poor; and we are to live for God and die to ourselves. Where the world says, "you must live for number one," Jesus says "what does it profit someone to gain the whole world and lose their soul?" Where society says, "become success-ful," Jesus defines success by humility—"the first will be last, the greatest will be the least, and the proud will be humbled." Where the world prioritizes knowledge and power, Jesus prizes simplic-ity and humility. Where the world is concerned with what we do, Jesus is concerned with who we are. Jesus is not safe because he teaches that discipleship in him flies in the face of all that the world teaches—and if you do not follow the values of the world, you will not be successful in the eyes of the world. Everything about Jesus and his kingdom is topsy-turvy and counterintuitive: Jesus was noble, but born in a barn; at his death, Jesus was a king with no fol-lowers, and he was a crucified messiah—a contradiction in terms.

The world, the unreflective Christian, and even the church have sought to domesticate Jesus, to make him tame and safe. But like Aslan, Jesus cannot be domesticated, manipulated, or controlled. We want to put Jesus on a leash. We seek to control him through prayer, doctrine, tradition, our churches, or what we believe about the Bible. But while all such things may be good, even God-given, at best they can only point to Jesus and his king-dom. Rather than trying to domesticate Jesus, we must learn to be silent until the roar of Jesus overcomes all other voices—our individualistic voices, and the self-centered voices of humanity. In this little book, I hope to remind the reader that we have failed to domesticate Jesus, simply because Jesus is beyond our tiny box-like thinking.

I have often heard people say things like, "believing your way is to step on a slippery slope; and slippery slopes are dangerous, they are to be avoided." But the kingdom of God is itself a slip-pery slope, and following Jesus necessarily includes confidently running upon a slippery slope. Avoiding the slippery slope is to avoid the kingdom. Because we like safety and security, we have the tendency to stay away from danger; but no such choice is given to the follower of Jesus. The teachings of Jesus are radical and dangerous, even as they produce inner peace and calm. People who avoid stepping on the slippery slope have been deceived by the world—for the world says, "follow me and all will be well," and Jesus says "following me means living in my dangerous kingdom."

How, it must be asked, has the world softened the message of Jesus? In the time of Jesus, it was the religious establishment that accused Jesus of being a disturber, a renegade, a blasphemer, and a false messiah. The religious authorities wanted security. They wanted control. They were threatened by anyone or any teaching that might challenge their security and control. Such religious authorities taught that challenging their power was to sin against God: living or teaching something that is contrary to Moses or to the traditions of the elders was to sin against God—and the religious authorities were alone the interpreters and stewards of Moses and the traditions. Making the people believe that disobeying the religious authorities was to disobey God was easy enough—for people also want security, and people will follow whatever power maintains their self-interests. What is true of the time of Jesus is equally true of today. In Jesus' day there were the Pharisees, the Sadducees, the Essenes, the Sanhedrin, the Zealots—and many other groups with different belief systems. The religious authorities of today are more diverse than at the time of Jesus. Today there are evangelicals, mainline Protestants, independents and non-denominationals, liberals and conservatives, charismatics and fundamentalists, Roman Catholics and Orthodox—and scores of other subgroups and persuasions. While they differ in many ways, such groups all claim allegiance to Jesus and his kingdom; and, like the religious authorities of old, they are all profoundly concerned with maintaining power—such that they regard any departure from their way of thinking as a departure from God. This is how they maintain power and control.

No doubt, there are beautiful Christians in every denomination—even as many folks in different persuasions at the time of Jesus truly wanted to follow God. One question that must concern us is, "How can we help such people?" The answer is not too complicated: we must encourage people to take their religious establishments with a grain of salt, not too seriously; we must encourage people to remember that all that counts is faith in Christ expressing itself in love. (I can hear protests: "This is just what my group does." But every group says this!) The problem is not with any one group or another, but with the attitude that one has in becoming a member of any group. The answer is not to avoid groups or denominations, for being in a group is mandatory: Christians need to go to church (the New Testament knows nothing about people having a "personal relationship with Jesus" outside of being in community). The answer is the attitude that one has in being a member of a church.

In this book I will explore the subject of Jesus being not safe. As with any book, one could easily go in a thousand different directions. The directions that I will explore are often academic; but this is not to say that my concerns are not practical. My concern is often with how poor thinking can lead one away from God, or good thinking can lead one toward God. If it is true that who we are and how we live is shaped by what we think, it is imperative that we think in a careful way. Part of the human condition is to complicate matters. In order to undo such complication and return to simplicity, it is often necessary to unwind the complexity. Doing so may involve cerebral activity, and so I apologize if this book seems to be complicated at points. All the same, I have confidence that the conclusions of this book have great bearing on discipleship in Jesus.

1

Believing Agnosticism

As with other chapters in this book, the title of this chapter is oxymoronic. In what sense is belief agnostic? By "agnostic" I am not in any way questioning the existence of God. The term *agnostic* simply means "against knowledge." One might say, "with respect to the conclusions of Eastern medicine, I am largely agnostic." Such a statement in no way challenges the conclusions of Eastern medicine. The person who utters this statement, rather, is aware that they do not have the mental wherewithal to challenge or accept the conclusions of Eastern medicine. The believing agnosticism of which I speak is belief in God that cannot be rigidly defined because it is beyond anyone's mental capacity to express it. Here is an allegory.

A stream meanders its way through pastoral land before making a rapid descent down a mountainside and past a village. At this point, the stream transforms everything that comes into its path: earth, pebbles, roots, and the terrain itself. Even though they know very little about other streams, the villagers who live along the banks of this stream boast that their stream is unparalleled in the world. As the stream winds its way through the valley, it merges with another stream. Without studying its contents, one might suppose that this other stream had a glacial source—for the stream is as clear as it is frigid. Just as soon as the two streams converge, they together become a river, and the distinctiveness that they each enjoyed prior to their union is at that point lost: a botanist might note that this or that cellular matter had its origin in the mountain stream because such matter exists only on the banks of that stream, even as a geologist might determine that a given pebble came from the glacial stream because, like the valley through which the glacial stream meanders, the pebble has volcanic features. Long after the two streams merge to become a river, the river itself merges into a wider river, which welcomes scores of other streams and rivers into itself. This wide river, in turn, empties into an ocean.

The stream made a rapid descent down the mountainside—such that it transformed everything in its path. This is akin to how the Western fascination with its particular understanding of rationality has foisted itself upon all other viewpoints, even as it has made itself the sole broker of any claim to truth. Something that fascinates me is the way in which Western Christians impose Western thinking upon the Bible—the very Bible that is replete with stories, declarations, and teaching that emphasize that human thinking is tiny and limited. That the truth of God is beyond human conceptualization is explicit in the following verse from the Old Testament.

> For my thoughts are not your thoughts, nor are your ways my ways, says the LORD.[1] For as the heavens are higher than the earth, so are my ways higher than your ways and my thoughts higher than your thoughts. (Isa 55:8–9)

Here is a similar declaration in the New Testament.

> O the depth of the riches and wisdom and knowledge of God! How unsearchable are his judgments and how inscrutable his ways! Who has known the mind of the Lord? Or who has been his counsellor? Who has ever

---

1. The term LORD indicates the divine name Yahweh.

given to God, that God should repay him? For from him
and through him and to him are all things. To him be the
glory forever. Amen. (Rom 11:33–36)

Paul similarly tells us that the nature of the afterlife surpasses
imagination, for in this life humanity can only know truth in part.

No eye has seen, nor ear heard, no mind has conceived,
what God has prepared for those who love him (1 Cor
2:9).

Now I know only in part; then I will know fully, even as I
have been fully known (1 Cor 13:12).

Because faith in Christ is not subject to rational proofs, it is
in the realm of the supra-rational. It follows that defending faith
as if it were subject to proof is wrongheaded. Throughout history
well-meaning individuals (mostly from the West) have sought to
defend the faith on a strictly rational basis. Most attempts to defend such faith have failed even before they began, for prior to
defending faith it is imperative to understand the nature of faith
itself. If one seeks to defend faith on the assumption that the truth
of faith may be ascertained on logical grounds, one has already
failed—for faith is outside the realm of proof. I thus have disregard
for books like *Evidence that Demands a Verdict* or *The Case for
Faith,* and many others besides. Such books are most embarrass-
ing—not simply because their authors are naive, but because such
books assume an understanding of faith that is altogether worldly.
The step from unbelief to belief must not be tied to the certainty of
faith, for faith involves personal encounter with God—not through
rational plausibility but through subjective longing.

In the preface to the second edition of his *Critique of Pure
Reason,* Immanuel Kant famously stated the following:

I must . . . abolish knowledge, to make room for belief.

As is clear from the context in which this statement appears, Kant is
not here denying that reason can make valid contributions to faith.
Kant's concern, rather, is to show that because reason can only

address matters that are outside the realm of faith, reason cannot create faith. Consistent with Kant's conclusion is the assertion that faith is based on supra-rational categories—categories that involve such matters as trusting God, growing in the love of God, and participating in the kingdom. As such, faith is not based on a host of arguments that are subject to logical verification. Approaching faith in the Western apologetic way is of little value—both because it uses categories that are alien to faith, and because, more practically, it is unsatisfying: in spite of cries to the contrary, the soul of humanity has little interest in proofs and much interest in peace of heart. History says, "Jesus was crucified"; and faith says, "Jesus was crucified for me." History says, "Jesus rose from the dead"; and faith says, "the resurrection of Jesus marked triumph over death." Philosophy says, "a first cause exists"; faith says, "I know the first cause as Father." A Christian apologetic that is bound to rationality is but a symptom of the Western mind's disease. (In referring to the Western mind's disease, I do not simply have in mind the eighteenth-century Enlightenment that prized human reason above all else, for human history is itself replete with hubris. Were we to rewrite the myth of Narcissus, it would not be humans loving their own reflection, but humans adoring their ability to reason.)

Akin to the way in which the mountain stream changed as it plummeted down the mountainside, minority voices have challenged Western thinking. Feminism, in particular, has contended that it is not so much the Western mind that is diseased, but the patriarchal Western mind—for with few exceptions the movers and shakers of the Western intellectual tradition have been male. Marxist philosophy has likewise contended that the Western mind has been diseased by power: much of the Western intellectual tradition has been shaped by people who have had a comfortable material existence, such that many of their concerns have been both elitist and impractical. Another voice that has challenged (and shaped) the Western mind is that of ethnic minorities. Just as the mountain stream merged with the glacial stream, in merging with the East, the Western intellectual tradition has likewise been forever changed. While the precise time in which these two traditions began to merge is unknown, whereas at the beginning of the twentieth century it might have been odd to welcome notions of Eastern thinking, doing so has since become commonplace.

Like the villagers in the allegory who boasted that their stream was unparalleled in the world, there is a certain smugness about the Western intellectual tradition, for it alone identifies and understands the complexities of knowledge and truth—such that the word-string "supra-rational truth" is off-putting, even offensive. But the majority of members of the non-Western world have had no problem in accepting the notion that truth might have a supra-rational element to it; indeed, as far back as recorded history takes us, we find that non-Western understandings of truth both begin and end with the assumption that truth surpasses human rationality. The ethnocentrism of the West is thus a very real problem: when humanity votes about how to know truth, it must not only consider the thinking of the West, for the less boisterous voice of the East must also be taken into account. The East has said a resounding No to the thinking of the West—such that much of its great literature assumes that truth is beyond that which can be rationally defended.

Different modern thinkers and Western schools of thought similarly show how the Western fascination with reason has unraveled. Blaise Pascal and Friedrich Nietzsche believed that rationality was unable to bring one to truth. Pascal viewed rationality with great suspicion: emotions, pride, vanity, and even cold weather, governed one's ability to reason. In all cases, issues of the heart trump reason. Pascal is well known for the following assertion:

The heart has its reasons of which reason knows nothing.[2]

Pascal similarly asserted that reason implodes upon itself, such that disregard of reason is most reasonable:

There is nothing so conformable to reason as this disavowal of reason.[3]

---

2. Pascal, *Pensées*, paragraph 277.
3. Pascal, *Pensées*, paragraph 272.

The last proceeding of reason is to recognize that there is
an infinity of things which are beyond it.[4]

Pascal's motivations behind his attack on reason were apologetic,
for he believed that an inflated understanding of reason lay behind
much unbelief. Like Pascal, Nietzsche contended that reason is unable to
assist one in finding truth—principally because rationality is subservient to the will to power. Nietzsche's disregard for rationalism
goes beyond that of Pascal, such that it would not be unfair to refer
to Nietzsche's philosophy as anti-rationalist. Nietzsche's disdain
for rationalism is itself implicit in the way that he argued, for his
writings are devoid of syllogistic logic and philosophical jargon—
the very tools of Western philosophers. While both Pascal and
Nietzsche abhorred the elevation of reason, and while they con-
curred that psychology trumps reason at every point, their regard
for psychology differed tremendously: whereas Pascal thought of
the heart's consistent triumph over rationality as a blow to rationality, Nietzsche celebrated this fact; and where Pascal lamented
that reason was subservient to pride, Nietzsche delighted that this
is the case—even implying that pride and the lust for power are
virtuous.

The emphasis of Pascal that all rationality is colored by emo-
tion and pride is akin to Kant's claim that things and ideas can only
be known subjectively, that is, through the human mind. While
such a view may seem to be hardly worthy of mention today, in the
eighteenth century the view that things are known only through
the filter of the individual mind was altogether scandalous. Kant's
assertion forever turned the world of philosophy on its head—such
that Kant's philosophy is likened to the Copernican Revolution.
The twentieth century produced two schools of thought that (like
Pascal, Kant, and Nietzsche) similarly challenged the primacy of
reason. The first was existentialism, which may simply be defined
in three words: "existence precedes essence." The concern of existentialism is that experiencing one's own life takes priority over

4. Pascal, Pensées, paragraph 267.

providing a conceptual model that may explain such life. The second school of thought that challenged the primacy of reason has been postmodernism, which holds that any conceptual framework that seeks to explain reality is inauthentic, for if absolutes exist, they are unknowable.[5]

In the allegory, the river welcomed other rivers and streams to itself prior to spilling into the ocean. This refers to the synthesizing of all life-giving human thought, which we have begun to see with the birth of the global community. While gross injustices of every type abound, human goodness abounds yet more. Never in history has there been less violence in the world per capita—whether it be violent crimes, crimes against women, war crimes, war itself, or violence against minorities, children, and even animals. Never before has the world seen a universal longing for a cessation to bigotry, tyranny, civil strife, and famine. Never before have there been so many non-governmental organizations that attend to the needs of the impoverished, the diseased, the starving, the illiterate, and refugees. Such growing philanthropy is due in part to the increase of democratic values and humanitarian concerns in much of the world—an increase that owes much to cosmopolitanism, development in education, and medical science.

The wide river spilling into an ocean concerns the way in which human goodness flows into divine goodness. At the river's mouth, fresh water mixes with salt water. So also, the disciple has one foot in the world of human goodness and, at the same time, one foot in the world of divine goodness. While existence in this in-between state is at times uncomfortable, people in this state can nevertheless confidently live—knowing that the ocean will prevail. It is at the convergence of the two waters where one sees the movement from rationality to supra-rationality. The existence of supra-rationality is not a flight from rationality. While for some it may be just that, for others supra-rationality naturally comes out of rationality itself—supra-rationality involves the suspension, not the negation, of rationality. Many people turn to supra-rationality

---

5. It has rightly been contended that postmodernism is little more than a footnote to the thinking of Nietzsche.

simply because they have seen that rationality can only take one so far down the river. When one has taken rationality as far as it can go, one may then become spiritually minded.

It is only a humanity that takes its rationality far too seriously that contends that belief is tied to certainty. Such a humanity wishes to marry mathematical formulae and syllogistic logic with belief. But a great problem is that mathematical formulae have nothing to do with the genuineness of belief. "One plus one equals two" applies only to rationalism and computers. This formula, true though it is, can say nothing about "one person plus one person may equal love." So also, the syllogism that says "all men are mortal; Socrates is a man; therefore Socrates is mortal" is altogether true—but as with math formulae, syllogistic thinking can say nothing about human affection, what is ethical, or what is beautiful. Only belief can describe such matters.

Most of what humanity holds dear is well beyond the boundaries of rationality. It is therefore surprising that people assert that for religion to be true it must be rational. But the same people who insist that religion can only be true if it is also rational are people who decry injustices—none of which can be defended on a strictly rational basis. Here is an analogy: A professor crosses a busy street before giving a lecture about how religion is untrue because it is not rational. On his way, this professor becomes incensed when a motorist cuts him off. The anger of the professor has little to do with rationality, but lots to do with his conviction that motorists *should* not behave this way. As soon as the idea of "should" is used, the professor has left the world of rationality and entered the world of the holy: the professor *dislikes* what the motorist did because the action of the motorist *threatened* the professor's lecture about the irrational nature of religion. Disregard for religion is itself religious. All the same, in order to legitimate itself, Western religion often tries to promote itself by saying that it is rational—for much of Western religion is only comfortable when it first pays allegiance to the god of Western thought, the god of rationality.

At its best, though, Western religions do not worship the god of reason. In their embracement of mystery, the three Western religions concur that God can be experienced, embraced, and loved. Such union with God is beautifully expressed in the poetry of Rumi. Here is but one of many examples.

> The Prophet said, "There are some who see me by the same light in which I am seeing them. Our natures are one. Without reference to any strands of lineage, without reference to texts or traditions, we drink the life-water together." Here's a story about the hidden mystery: The Chinese and the Greeks were arguing as to who were the better artists. The king said, "We'll settle this matter with a debate." The Chinese began talking, but the Greeks wouldn't say anything. They left. The Chinese suggested then that they each be given a room to work on with their artistry, two rooms facing each other and divided by a curtain. The Chinese asked the king for a hundred colours, all the variations, and each morning they came to where the dyes were kept and took them all. The Greeks took no colours. "[Such colours are] no part of our work [they said]." [The Greeks] went to their room and began cleaning and polishing the walls. All day every day they made those walls as pure and clear as an open sky. . . . The Chinese finished, and they were so happy. They beat the drums in the joy of completion. The king entered their room, astonished by the gorgeous colours and detail. The Greeks then pulled the curtain dividing the rooms. The Chinese figures and images shimmeringly reflected on the clear Greek walls. They lived there, even more beautifully, and always changing in the light. The Greek art is the sufi way. [The sufis] don't study books of philosophical thought. They make their loving clearer and clearer. No wantings, no anger. In that purity they receive and reflect the images of every moment, from here, from the stars, from the void. They take them in as though they were seeing with the lighted clarity that sees them.[6]

There is nothing in this poem to suggest that union with God is only for those who are philosophically minded, steeped in Scripture, or given to a formal life of prayer and devotion. This

---

6. Barks, ed., *Rumi*, 121–22.

is a huge mistake. Rumi makes fun of such people: "the mystic flies moment to moment; the fearful ascetic drags along month to month."[7] Rumi's contention is parallel to a prayer of the celebrated mystic, Theresa of Avila: "from silly devotions and from sour-faced saints, good Lord, deliver us." Union with God has little to do with spiritual intoxication or divine ecstasy, and it has everything to do with living a simple life of love.

All human love points beyond itself to the love of God—such that human love is purest when it is grounded in the love of God, even as love for God is purest when it spills over into love for people. The two loves are inseparably one. For those who have eyes to see, so-called mundane love always points to supra-mundane love. Pure love between parent and child, between spouse and spouse, and between friend and stranger is based on the inner awareness that God (however he might be defined) is love. It matters not if the love comes from a rabbi, a priest, an imam, a heretic, or even a self-declared atheist—for words can be clumsy and cheap. Supra-rational faith, which spans the three great Western religions in diverse forms, speaks to the simple the message of love.

Perhaps the subject of mystery can be best explored with regard to how the name of God has been understood. With reference to Judaism, the way in which God disclosed his name to Moses is most telling. While Moses was keeping the flock, God appeared to him, told Moses to take off his shoes as he was standing on holy ground, and identified himself as the God of the patriarchs. God then told Moses that he was going to deliver the Hebrews from slavery in Egypt and bring them into the promised land. At this point in the narrative, God disclosed his name to Moses:

> Moses said to God, "If I come to the Israelites and say to them, 'The God of your ancestors has sent me to you,' and they ask me, 'What is his name?' what shall I say to them?" God said to Moses, "I am who I am." He said further, "Thus you shall say to the Israelites, 'I am has sent me to you.'" God also said to Moses, "Thus you shall say to the Israelites, 'The LORD, the God of your ancestors,

---

7. Barks, ed., *Rumi*, 179.

the God of Abraham, the God of Isaac, and the God of
Jacob, has sent me to you: this is my name forever, and
this my title for all generations.'" (Exod 3:13–15)

God's disclosure of his name, "I am who I am"—which is a
play on the Hebrew verb "to be"—needs to be understood in light
of the ancient Near East where knowing the name of the deity
could enable one to have some control over the deity. Equally true
is the fact that names often denoted character: Moses knew that
people would want to know the name of God so that they would
know the character of this God. God's answer to Moses's demand
to know God's name is therefore both a subtle rebuke as well as an
answerless answer: a subtle rebuke insofar as one should not dare
to manipulate or control God; and an answerless answer insofar as
"I am who I am" may be paraphrased as "I am whomever I choose
to be, so do not try to pin me down."

With regard to Islam, the so-called ninety-nine names of
God have had a central role to play.[8] Here are two references in the
Koran to the names of God.

Call upon Allah or call upon the Most Merciful. Which-
ever you call—to Him belong the best names. (17:110)

Allah! there is no God but He! To Him belong the Most
Beautiful Names. (20:8)

While the ninety-nine names of God aid the worshipper in
understanding the nature of God, there is no suggestion that all
such names do complete justice to who God is, for God transcends
all human language and thought forms. Similarly, while the ninety-nine names of God are instructive, they are not perfect encap-
sulations of who God is. In a strict sense, all that finite humans can
do is say what God is not.

With reference to Christianity, the name of God is both unknowable and knowable all at once: unknowable insofar as no one

8. I say "so-called" because more than ninety-nine names of God exist in
the Koran and the sunnah. There are, moreover, discrepancies between authoritative lists of the ninety-nine names.

has seen God, but knowable insofar as God has been seen in the Son. Although at a certain level the Christian dares not try to describe God, the Christian is nevertheless free to describe the Son. Consistent with this, early Christians equated the unknowable name of God with the knowable name of Jesus. An instance of this paradox may be seen in the close of the *kenōsis* hymn:

> Therefore God also highly exalted him and gave him the name that is above every name, so that at the name of Jesus every knee should bend, in heaven and on earth and under the earth, and every tongue should confess that Jesus Christ is Lord, to the glory of God the Father (Phil 2:9–11).

While it is clear that "the name that is above every name" is the name Jesus, "the name that is above every name" is an allusion to the name of God. This interpretation is supported by the fact that this text in Philippians is a quotation of God's declaration in Isaiah: "to me every knee shall bow, every tongue shall swear" (Isa 45:23). Such equating of the name Jesus with the name of the God of Israel is equally present in the "I am" sayings of the Gospel of John. Here is one such saying:

> Your ancestor Abraham rejoiced that he would see my day; he saw it and was glad. Then the Jews said to him, "You are not yet fifty years old, and have you seen Abraham?" Jesus said to them, "Very truly, I tell you, before Abraham was, I am." So they picked up stones to throw at him, but Jesus hid himself and went out of the temple. (John 8:56–59)

Various religious leaders were incensed with what they thought was a suggestion that Jesus saw Abraham; but they were altogether infuriated when Jesus went further in his declaration that "before Abraham was, I am"—for in this declaration Jesus not only alluded to his pre-existence, but he also suggested that he was somehow one with the God of Israel—the "I am" who appeared to Moses in the burning bush. The unknowable God is known in Jesus, for Jesus is the perfect human expression of God.

With reference to the name of God in Eastern religions, one must be very careful—simply because most Eastern religions neither affirm nor deny the existence of God. Some might, therefore, find it odd to speak of how Eastern religions speak of the name of God. But if, with Paul Tillich, one equates "God" with matters of "ultimate concern," Eastern religion readily finds a place in "name of God" discourse. The Eastern religion of Taoism, in particular, teaches something wonderful about the name. Here are two lines from the Tao Te Ching.

> The way that can be named is not the eternal Way (Tao Te Ching, poem 1).

> I do not know its name, except to call it Tao (Tao Te Ching, poem 25).

In Taoist thought, because truth is beyond rational definition, any claim to truth must not adhere to definitions. Truth is to be lived and experienced for it to be known.[9]

Given that great challenges to Western reasoning have come both from within itself and from the East, it may come as a surprise that rationality continues to be placed high upon a pedestal. This vaunting of rationality stems from the insecurity of the human condition: because individuals long for certainty, they are compelled to place rationality above all else. But apart from mathematics, syllogistic reasoning, and death, certainty about anything is a myth; yet as elusive as certainty might be, people grasp for it. Faith must not be confused with certainty, even as doubt must not be confused with unbelief. Being happily agnostic is a key element of faith. Whereas certainty involves cognitive assurance, agnostic belief involves embracing and being embraced. Disciples of Jesus

---

9. Parallels between a Christian understanding of the "Word" and a Taoist understanding of the "Way" are delightful: the Word or the Way undergirds all existence; the Word or the Way has made itself known through humility; and disciples find their identity in becoming expressions of the Word or the Way. A fundamental difference between the Word and the Way concerns relationship: in Christian thought, the Word became human and therefore relational; in Taoist thought, the Way is impersonal.

allow room for uncertainty within their faith, for they know that to the degree that their faith does not leave room for uncertainty their faith is disingenuous—for uncertainty is a core element of what it means to be human. Even as God is greater than our beliefs, God is greater than our doubts. The faithful likewise tell themselves that insofar as they are uncomfortable with uncertainty, they doubt the goodness of God, for faith in God surpasses the certain versus uncertain dichotomy: "if we are faithless, God will remain faithful, for he cannot disown himself" (2 Tim 2:13). People do not know God because they are certain about the truth of God; rather, they are both known by God and they know God because they have encountered him through faith. Using an example from my own life, I do not believe that my wife loves me because I know that she exists, but I believe that she loves me because she affirms me. The subject of certainty has nothing to do with our relationship, a relationship that is founded on reciprocating affection for one another. So it is with God. God loves me, this I know, not because I can prove that he exists, but because I experience his goodness.

Does rationality have a role to play in thinking about religion? Most certainly. I recently had a conversation with a university student about God. As is typical, she said that the existence of God cannot be proven. I reminded her that we cannot prove most of the things that we believe: we cannot prove that anything is beautiful; we cannot prove that music can enrich us; we cannot prove that humans have rights; and we cannot prove that it is best to be kind, generous, loving, or fair. But we believe in such things, and many more things as well—things that we cannot begin to prove, even things for which we might die. I also told her that the debate over the existence of God is akin to two fish in a bowl in which one fish tells the other that it will not believe in the existence of water unless it can be proven that water exists. The fact is that the ocean of life is awash with the presence of God (however "God" might be defined), and, like the unbelieving fish, it is rather silly to debate whether God exists. All the same, I told the student that while one cannot "prove" the existence of God, it is much more rational to believe in the existence of God than to believe in his nonexistence.

I told the student that while there have been many arguments given over the centuries concerning the existence of God, the argument from cosmology (which itself consists of many arguments) is most convincing. It simply boils down to this: What is more rational, to believe that the universe came from nothing or to believe that something outside of time and space created all things? Without exception, all science—whether at the microscopic or macroscopic levels—is based on cause and effect. Is is rational to believe that the big bang was causeless? Surely not. This requires more faith than what a fundamentalist believer could ever muster. The student agreed with me. She said that she, too, believed that something greater than time and space started all things. Her problem was referring to this Starter as God. I told her that language is clumsy, and that "God" is the word that we use to refer to this Starter. I then went on to tell her that while there is a place for rationality, we can only begin with belief: we believe in order that we might understand—not vice versa. I told here that the principal function of rationality in the life of faith is to generate humility within the believer: by knowing that life cannot be understood only rationally, we pave the way for humility—and believing agnosticism is nothing less than an extension of humility to the mind.

The reader might suspect that my emphasis on the relative impotence of rationality is partially due to my fascination with Eastern religious thinking. This suspicion is correct. But this fascination has nothing to do with imposing Eastern forms of thought on Christian theology. The simple fact is that Christian history is itself chock-full of individuals, books, and schools of thought that have sought to bring reason down from its lofty pedestal. One thinks of Tertullian, who famously asked, "What does Jerusalem have to do with Athens?" One thinks of Anselm, who said, "I believe in order that I might understand." So also, one reading *The Cloud of Unknowing* cannot help but see the tremendous overlap between its counsel and the teaching of Zen Buddhism. While various individuals, books, and schools of thought have challenged the traditional place that Christianity has given to rationalism, none of them have sought to undermine the need for rational thought. Indeed, the very challenge to rationalism is itself rational. One cannot escape the need for rationality. The question is one of degree. What is true of Christian theology is also true of Eastern religious thought. The Eastern religion that is most dubious about rationality is Zen Buddhism. According to Zen, much of suffering is the consequence of falling prey to wandering thoughts—but mastering wandering thoughts is itself a thought, such that rationality is unavoidable. The Tao Te Ching also concerns itself with the clumsy nature of words, but it uses thousands of words (eighty-one chapters) to say as much! The human condition is such that humanity must use words to express belief. But belief is not a slave to words. Trying to encapsulate God in words is, in fact, symptomatic of the sin of idolatry.

2

Benign Idolatries

Modifying the word *idolatries* with the word *benign* might seem self-contradictory, for it is rightly thought that idolatry can never be good. But the sin of idolatry comes as close as one can get to having a good sin, for behind all idolatry there exists a longing to pay devotion to the Ultimate. (Perhaps the word "urge" is better than "longing," for the sin of idolatry is as impulsive as it is unreflective.) When the Israelites built the golden calf, they said, "These are your gods, O Israel, who brought you up from the land of Egypt" (Exod 32:4). It presumably did not occur to the Israelites that they were sinning, for their intention was simply to honor the One who delivered them from Egypt. In many instances of ancient Hebrew idolatry, it was similarly not a matter of worshipping a god other than the God of Israel, but failing to distinguish between an image of God and the God of Israel himself. The sin of idolatry involves misplaced affections—adoring what points to God more than God himself. Here we have the corruption of the best that leads to the worst.

The corruption of the best that leads to the worst particularly raises its head in the field of religion with its Scriptures, doctrines, and traditions. Scripture, doctrine, and tradition are all good—insofar as they point to God. But endemic to the human condition is the tendency to absolutize what points to the Absolute. I am here reminded of a common motif in Buddhist legend in which a distinction is to be made between the moon (the Absolute) and the finger that points to the moon. In one such legend, a Zen master goes for a walk one evening with one of his disciples. The disciple, who was presumably taken aback by this tremendous honor, flooded the master with a host of esoteric questions: "What is the nature of Nirvana?" "What is reality?" "Does every individual have a soul?" Seeing that the disciple was preoccupied with concepts rather than existence itself, without verbally answering the master simply pointed to the moon. Through this simple gesture, the disciple became aware that one must make a distinction between opinions about the Absolute and the Absolute itself: the finger is but a pointer to the moon—it is not the moon itself. Insofar as we fixate on what points to the moon, we fail both in appreciating the function of the pointer and in appreciating the moon. The history of religious thought is riddled with the disciple's problem, for those things that exist to point to the Absolute become absolutized themselves. We analyze features of the finger: its scars, the way that the veins intertwine the muscles, and the particularities of the finger's print; but all along we fail to attend to the principal function of the finger—the finger is pointing beyond itself. In Christian history, the failure to look beyond the pointer to the Absolute is particularly seen in how the Bible, doctrine, and tradition have functioned.

Since the Protestant Reformation of the sixteenth century, the understanding of the nature and function of the Bible in the life of faith has been predominant. Together with *sola fide* (faith alone) and *sola gratis* (grace alone), the Reformers emphasized *sola scriptura* (the Bible alone). The Bible was thought to contain everything that was necessary for salvation and the life of holiness. In the centuries since the Reformation, questions concerning the nature and authority of the Bible have had a central role to play in Protestant faith. Even in the time of the Reformers, disagreements abounded concerning how the Bible is to be interpreted, its relationship to tradition, and whether it is appropriate to subscribe to any beliefs that were not explicitly condoned in the Bible (e.g., the use of musical instruments in worship). Without leaving such questions behind, the seventeenth century saw a more particular emphasis on systematizing the Bible. If, it was thought, the Bible alone has all the answers of religion, it behooves the believing community to systematize the truth of the Bible. Topics included the nature of divine revelation, the nature of God, the nature of humanity, the nature of salvation, the person and work of Christ, the nature of the church, and the nature of last things. Put on the back burner were concerns with wonder, faithfulness, the spiritual life, encounter with God, and the human condition. For all too many Christians, the Bible had become a source book, a divine encyclopaedia that is to be systematized so that the truth of God might be understood and explained.

The eighteenth century brought with it a painful, but needed, corrective to the scholasticism of the seventeenth century. The so-called Enlightenment that began with this century taught that far from being a divine word, the Bible consisted of a hodgepodge of ancient Semitic and Graeco-Roman religious thought. It was thought to be superstitious to think otherwise. While still fighting among themselves over precisely how the Bible was to be understood, many churchmen and scholars turned their attention to defending the divine nature of the Bible. The nineteenth century saw a continuation of Enlightenment attacks and defenses of the Bible. One factor that furthered the argument was the archaeologist's spade: with new discoveries of ancient literature, there came a greater understanding and appreciation of the general worldviews of the ancient mind—worldviews that are often the very inverse of the modern mind. Defending the divine nature of the Bible became an increasingly difficult task as more and more evidence suggested that the authors and editors of Bible presupposed very different understandings of reality than those that are embraced in the modern world. Largely because of the onslaught of Enlightenment thought (and the birth of modern archaeology), an inevitable fracturing within the North American version of Protestantism developed in the early twentieth century. Whereas liberal Protestantism sought to define itself with reference to the raging "Babel vs. Bible" controversy that already started in the mid-nineteenth century, conservative Protestantism regarded such acquiescence as most problematic. As the "Babel vs. Bible" controversy evolved and carried with it Darwinian and then Freudian thought, the conservative wing of Protestantism itself divided between the fundamentalists and the evangelicals—the primary difference between the two being fundamentalism's outright disregard and evangelicalism's general tolerance for modern thought.

The enmity, discord, and argumentation within Protestantism since the time of the Reformers has largely been the unwitting consequence of attempting to absolutize what is relative, of failing to distinguish between what points to the moon and the moon itself. The Bible is a pointer to divine reality. Absolutizing it in some that way constitutes a benign idolatry: "benign" in the sense that reading, studying, and meditating on the Bible is laudatory (doing so can bring great life); but "idolatrous" in the sense that love for the Bible and the truth that it contains often constitutes a misapplied affection—the Christian is to love God and neighbor, not a book that points to love for God and neighbor. Misplacing love for God and neighbor with preoccupation with the contents of a book that pertains to love for God and neighbor is a toxic mistake.

Examples in the Old Testament of such misapplied affections are many. Presumably with a mocking tone, Isaiah castigated religious leaders for focusing on the correct interpretation of an authoritative teaching.

> For it is precept upon precept, precept upon precept, line upon line, line upon line, here a little, there a little. (Isa 28:10)

That such authoritative teaching was based on a malleable tradition is suggested in the next chapter where the Lord said the following through Isaiah.

> These people come near to me with their mouth and honour me with their lips, but their hearts are far from me. Their worship of me is based on merely human rules they have been taught. (Isa 29:13)

The temptation to absolutize the pointer is also seen in the way in which religious matters might eclipse love for neighbor. More specifically, the prophets often spoke against religion that is devoid of compassion and social justice. Here is a prophecy from Amos.

> I hate, I despise your festivals, and I take no delight in your solemn assemblies. Even though you offer me your burnt offerings and grain offerings, I will not accept them; and the offerings of well-being of your fatted animals I will not look upon. Take away from me the noise of your songs; I will not listen to the melody of your harps. But let justice roll down like waters, and righteousness like an ever-flowing stream. (Amos 5:21–24)

Here are similar prophecies from Isaiah.

> What to me is the multitude of your sacrifices? says the LORD; I have had enough of burnt offerings of rams and the fat of fed beasts; I do not delight in the blood of bulls, or of lambs, or of goats. When you come to appear before me, who asked this from your hand? Trample my courts no more; bringing offerings is futile; incense is an abomination to me. New moon and sabbath and calling of convocations—I cannot endure solemn assemblies with iniquity. Your new moons and your appointed festivals my soul hates; they have become a burden to me, I am weary of bearing them. When you stretch out your hands, I will hide my eyes from you; even though you make many prayers, I will not listen; your hands are full of blood. Wash yourselves; make yourselves clean; remove the evil of your doings from before my eyes; cease to do evil, learn to do good; seek justice, rescue the oppressed, defend the orphan, plead for the widow. (Isa 1:11–17)

> Look, you fast only to quarrel and to fight and to strike with a wicked fist. Such fasting as you do today will not make your voice heard on high. Is such the fast that I choose, only a day to humble oneself? Is it only for bowing one's head like a reed and for lying in sackcloth and ashes? Will you call this a fast, a day acceptable to the

LORD? Is not this the fast that I choose: to loose the bonds
of injustice, to undo the thongs of the yoke, to let the oppressed go free, and to break every yoke? Is it not to share
your bread with the hungry, and bring the homeless poor
into your house; when you see the naked, to cover them,
and not to hide yourself from your own kin? (Isa 58:4–7)

The Gospels are themselves replete with denunciations of the
tendency to absolutize Scripture or tradition at the expense of true
religion. Such denunciations are often present in the teaching of
Jesus—whether it be the way in which he castigated various Pharisees for "straining out a gnat but swallowing a camel" in the seven
woes (Matt 23), or the way that he denounced the love of tradition
when it became more important than the love of people (e.g., Matthew 15:1–19). Jesus could say to religious folks: "You have a fine
way of rejecting the commandment of God in order to keep your
tradition!" (Mark 7:9).

It would be a huge mistake, however, to think that Jesus repu-
diated Scripture itself. Jesus' problem was not with Scripture, but
with the abuse of Scripture—more specifically, failing to see that
Scripture pointed beyond itself to God, to Jesus himself, and to
the kingdom of God. It was with this in mind that Jesus repeatedly
said, "and now something greater is here."

At that time Jesus went through the grain fields on the
sabbath; his disciples were hungry, and they began to
pluck heads of grain and to eat. When the Pharisees saw
it, they said to him, "Look, your disciples are doing what
is not lawful to do on the sabbath." He said to them, "Have
you not read what David did when he and his companions were hungry? He entered the house of God and ate
the bread of the Presence, which it was not lawful for him
or his companions to eat, but only for the priests. Or have
you not read in the law that on the sabbath the priests
in the temple break the sabbath and yet are guiltless? I
tell you, *something greater than* the temple is here. . . .
The people of Nineveh will rise up at the judgment with
this generation and condemn it, because they repented
at the proclamation of Jonah, and see, *something greater*

than Jonah is here! The queen of the South will rise up
at the judgment with this generation and condemn it,
because she came from the ends of the earth to listen to
the wisdom of Solomon, and see, *something greater than
Solomon is here!* (Matt 12:1–6; 41–42)

Whether, then, it was the holy temple, the prophet Jonah, or king
Solomon—all alike pointed beyond themselves to something
greater, and disciples of the kingdom are not to lose sight of this
"something" by being preoccupied with things that point to it.

What I said above regarding the golden calf of Protestant
idolatry, the Bible itself, is equally true of misapplied devotion to
doctrine—simply because the backbone of all doctrine in Protestantism has been the Bible. By all means, let doctrine be shaped
and defined by the Bible; but insofar as such doctrine is based on
an understanding that the Bible is absolute, such doctrine is flim-
sy—for then doctrine is no better than a house built on sand. Painful examples abound. I think, for example, of the controversy of a
bygone era over whether humans are bipartite (consisting of body
and soul), or whether they are tripartite (consisting of body, mind,
and soul). Any dogmatic answer to this question that is based on
the Bible can only begin with the naive assumption that the sixty-
six books of the Bible are in agreement on this point, and the very
question contains within itself seeds of self-destruction—for the
Bible has no concern whatever in any of its parts to address such
impractical matters.

Precisely how tradition can be a benign idolatry differs from
how the Bible or doctrine can feed idolatry—for unlike the Bible
and doctrine, tradition often concerns how one worships. I here
think of various liturgical traditions within Roman Catholicism,
Anglicanism, and Orthodoxy—traditions that originally had a
thoroughly pragmatic function but later bore sacramental significance. Take the altar rail, for example. The original function of
the rail was to keep domesticated animals away from the altar so
that they would not consume the bread and wine. But over time
a whole theology crept into what was originally only a pragmatic
matter: "why yes," it was thought, "there should be a fence around

the altar as this implies that a distinction is to be made between the priest and the laity"; and "yes, the altar rail is low so that the worshipper must kneel (a gesture of humility and repentance) in order to receive the consecrated elements." And what of the priest's collar? It is nothing more than what a gentleman in Roman times would wear—perhaps even as one might wear a tie today. Over time, however, even as the societal vogue changed, churchmen (who often take themselves far too seriously) opted to retain the custom of wearing the collar, such that only clerics wore the collar—the rest of society had moved on. What is true of the Roman collar is equally true of various vestments. As an Anglican pastor, every Sunday I put on my alb and over it I placed my stole. Originally, the alb was worn by monks simply to keep them warm, and what we call a stole was nothing more than a scarf. But as with the Roman collar, such mundane garments began to clothe themselves with theological significance. Whether it is the collar or the vestments that a priest wears during the sacred service, the implied message is inescapable: "those who wear such garments are particularly important, for they are special agents of God."

(It is not as if non-liturgical Christian denominations are above elevating the mundane. While I was a Baptist missionary in Nigeria, the church that I attended in my village was modest in every respect—it was made with mud blocks and tin. I was taken aback, however, with its pulpit, which was was elevated, enclosed with a rail and gate, and decorated with a garland. While such embellishments may, in part, be explained by colonial influence, they may equally be explained by the human tendency to elevate the mundane. The elevation of the mundane is particularly seen in the faddishness of contemporary evangelicalism: whether it be a new perspective on evangelism or spiritual warfare, a spate of self-help books dealing with a particular issue, a style of worship, the teaching of one pastor or another [often from a "megachurch"], or a big-screen movie, evangelicalism [not unlike consumerist society] excels in absolutizing fads that disappear as quickly as they appear. This faddishness is akin to the movement of a butterfly, which incessantly flits about from one object of interest to another. Where a trap for liturgical churches exists in regarding one tradition or another as an end in itself, as a consequence of their effort to avoid tradition, evangelicalism often falls prey to an opposite trap: absolutizing the ephemeral.)

In addition to the metaphor of confusing the pointer with what it points to, there is the metaphor of confusing the map with the territory. Maps exist only to assist people in understanding a particular territory—be they topographical maps, astronomical maps, or road maps. It would be peculiar indeed if a person had a great knowledge of a road map but had no corresponding interest in travelling through its territory. Society would be right in suggesting that such an individual is strange. But treating the Bible, doctrine, or tradition as ends in themselves is not much different than regarding a map as an end in itself. Is doing so not neurotic at some level? Perhaps. But unbelieving society cannot here judge the believer, simply because this would amount to the pot calling the kettle black—for unbelieving society is itself driven by a legion of meaningless pursuits. The fact is that all humanity alike is prone to confuse the pointer with the Absolute. I am reminded of a picture that I recently saw of Buddhist monks—all of whom would have been well aware of the common motif in the sutras concerning failure to distinguish between the pointer and the Absolute. In the picture the monks were paying homage to a relic of Buddha's finger!

3

The Bible as a Pointer

In the previous chapter, I spoke of how humans absolutize pointers to the Absolute. This is particularly true of how the Bible has been understood. Because I introduced this matter in only a cursory way, in this chapter I will discuss the question more fully. My concern throughout this chapter is not to deprecate the Bible in any way, but to underscore the fact that it points to God.

The absolutization of the Bible started to take place when the individual scrolls that make up the Bible were thought to be different than other literature—there was something God-given about them. This happened at different times for different scrolls. In the time of Jesus, the Hebrew Bible (the Christian Old Testament) consisted of three sections: the Law, the Prophets, and the Writings. The Law included the five books of Moses.[1] The Prophets were divided into two groups: the former prophets (Isaiah, Jeremiah, and Ezekiel), and the latter prophets (Hosea—Malachi). The Writings were works that had varying statuses within the Jewish community: some of the Writings were regarded as Scripture,

---

1. The title "Law" is unfortunate as it implies that the Books of Moses (also called the Pentateuch) are legal in nature. While many parts of these books are legal, much of them consist of narratives—stories concerning early humanity, the patriarchs, and the birth of Israel. But because the title "Law" has been used since ancient times, I am compelled to use this designation—inexact though it may be.

others were not, and still others were in the process of being regarded as Scripture. While the Law had been regarded as Scripture for centuries (certainly by the fifth-century BCE), it itself consists of many different sources that had been pieced together over the centuries. The many scrolls that made up the Law were at one time also separate from each other. They were only regarded as Scripture after such scrolls were united.

What is true of the Law is also true of the Prophets. The prophetic scrolls were at one time independent of each other. As each of them became more respected, they took on increasing authority—such that they eventually were regarded as Scripture. At some point, the prophetic writings were themselves also grouped together: this is particularly clear from the twelve latter prophets, which were together referred to as "the Book of the Twelve."

Precisely how the Writings took on Scriptural status differed. While some of the Writings (e.g., Psalms) were universally regarded as being Scripture, others had to vie for scriptural status. Communities, groups, and individuals had different opinions regarding the scriptural status of one or another scroll. Every scroll had a different story: with regard to the Psalms, there was a discussion about whether Psalm 151 should be included; and like Esther, the Song of Songs does not even mention God—and it is love poetry (even erotic in places), so it certainly must not be regarded as Scripture.

Similar disagreements regarding the scriptural status of different books exist today. While all Christians regard the same sixty-six books of the Bible as Scripture, many disagree as to the scriptural status of the deuterocanonical or apocryphal books.[2] The Roman Catholics have their extra books, as do the Orthodox, and the Coptics. The absolutization of every work in the Bible was furthered when the sixty-six books of the Bible became a single book. Prior to the fifth-century AD, the Bible consisted of dozens

---

2. This was equally true of the early Christian movement, for even here there was disagreement over what books are scriptural. (The book of Jude, for example, quotes both *The Assumption of Moses* and *The Book of Enoch* as though both books were Scripture.)

of separate scrolls; but with the invention of the binding of books, the Bible's separate works became a single book. Once individual works were regarded as Scripture, it became relatively easy to further this belief for every book of the Bible—for the question now was not if one or another book was Scripture, but if the whole collection of books was Scripture.

Having discussed the historical movement from individual scroll to unified book, I will now consider the felt need for Scripture.[3] The felt need for Scripture is the desire that people have for a definite and specific understanding of what God wants. The thinking is that if they have this definite understanding, they will be more able to follow God. But this is only a felt need; it is not a genuine need. We only feel the need for absolute Scripture because we lack faith. The more that our faith grows, the less we need a book (however God-given it may be) to guide us in our lives. What the Christian must learn to follow is that "still, small voice" within them—the voice of the Spirit, the voice of conscience, the voice of the love of God in Jesus. I am here reminded of many people who have asked me what God's will is. With the best of intentions, such people are hoping that I might produce for them a single Bible verse or a collection of such verses that would give them direction. In response to their query (and perhaps to their dismay), I often tell a story about St. Augustine: Someone asked the saint what God's will was, and he simply told them, "Love God and do what you want." The reasoning here is that if you prioritize love for God, then whatever you decide to do will be pleasing to him. Looking in the Bible to find the specific will of God is really no different than studying the stars to know one's fate, or looking at an animal's liver to determine the will of the gods. What is needed is simple trust that is guided by love for God.

In the sphere of religion, security can be found in belief systems. If we believe the correct things, or so we think, then we can be on God's side; if we are in the right church, then we might be on God's side; if we worship the proper way, then we may well be

---

3. I say "felt need" carefully, for we often deceive ourselves by thinking that our wants are needs.

on God's side; if we have been baptized and we go to mass, then we are on God's side; or if we have a "personal relationship" with Jesus, then we are certainly on God's side. This longing for security in the area of religion similarly manifests itself in the felt need for Scripture: if we live according to the Bible, then we can be on God's side. Coupled with security is the desire for control—if we can control our environment, then we can be more sure that our environment is secure. With regard to the Bible, it is not just reading it that gives us religious security, for we must interpret it in the right way—and communities of faith tell us how to interpret the Bible in the right way. Liturgical churches tell us that the only true interpretation of the Bible that pleases God is the one that their tradition has provided. So-called conservative Christians similarly tell us to go to any church, but it must be "Bible-believing" (that is, a church that understands everything in the Bible their way—talking snakes and the like). Religion thus tells us how to read and interpret the Bible—thereby giving us greater control and security.

The felt need for Scripture also assumes that people can read. We are, presumably, to think that there is a definite relationship between experiencing the mercy of God and knowing the contents of a book. Can people only follow God if they themselves are literate or if they know someone who can explain the sacred literature to them? If we believed this, than we would not believe in mercy— for God's kindness and generosity to us would then be based on our ability. For thousands of years before and after Christ, people embraced truth simply because God had put such truth in their hearts—not because they could read a book about God. No doubt, the Bible has helped people immensely in their understanding of God, but the suggestion that the mercy of God is somehow tied to literacy is most problematic. Christians rightly believe that people should read the Bible. Christians also rightly believe that the Bible is the only historical document that speaks about Jesus, the person through whom the world can experience salvation. But it is a careless non sequitur from this to saying that people must know about a book before they can experience salvation—simply because the truth of the Bible is way beyond its pages. The Bible points to truth.

It does not tightly hold on to truth, such that truth can only be known if one understands the Bible in the right way.

Despite cries to the contrary, the felt need for Scripture is worldly. The modern view that Scripture is somehow perfect is little more than the spiritualization of Enlightenment thinking, which asserts that perfection is consistent, unified, and historically sound. (I am here reminded of the oft-quoted statement of Emerson: "A foolish consistency is the hobgoblin of little minds, adored by little statesmen and philosophers and divines.") As I noted in an earlier chapter, the so-called Enlightenment of the eighteenth century was a time in which Western humanity concluded that everything must be judged by human rationality. Religion was regarded as superstitious because its doctrines could not be proven. To defend itself, the church did its utmost to show that Scripture was somehow perfect. The problem is that the church used Enlightenment thinking to defend itself against Enlightenment thinking. The church thus lost the battle even before it began its defense.

The defense of Scripture along Enlightenment modes of thinking led to a circus of silly interpretations of the Bible, even as such defenses strove to define precisely what it meant when it said that the Bible was inerrant or infallible. Here are some of the conclusions. Yes, the personalities who wrote much of the Bible are reflected in their writings, but God nevertheless directed ("superintended") them to ensure that his infallible will would be recorded. No, we don't have any original manuscripts, but we can be sure that what we have is close to the original. By "inerrant," we really don't mean without error but only without error with respect to religious matters (for we know that the Bible is replete with historical and scientific errors). Perhaps, or so it was thought, rather than using the word "inerrant" we should use the word "infallible"—for this word allows one to believe that while the Bible may have errors, the inclusion of such errors reflects the fact that God used fallible humanity to create his infallible book.

Contrary to all of this clamor, the concern of the Bible is not how one should or should not think about it. The concern is with trust in God, a trust that is fulfilled in love for God and neighbor.

We must love God, not a book that points to God. Such answers were not acceptable to many in the church, who insisted that their holy book must somehow be perfect. But only God is perfect, and only God is inerrant, infallible, and absolute. Thinking otherwise is, at best, to pollute a pure faith with worldly thinking. At worst, thinking otherwise may be idolatrous—or even unbelieving.

It is clear that, far from being absolute perfection, the many parts of the Bible have an evolutionary history—much of which can be traced. Any honest reading of the Bible would note that the ethical standards of the God of the Bible changed over time. This evolution is nowhere more apparent than between the counsel of the psalmist and that of Jesus: the psalmist could say that one is blessed if he kills baby Babylonians by smashing their heads against a rock (Ps 137:9), and Jesus could beckon the little children to come and be blessed by him (Matt 19:14). The God of the Old Testament likewise told people to commit murder and genocide: he told Abraham to slay his son; he told the Israelites to slaughter the Canaanites; he told Moses to burn alive homosexuals and to stone blasphemers; he told Saul to utterly destroy everything that the Amalekites owned—including babes and domesticated animals. There are many other atrocities that God sanctioned in the Old Testament. Rather than baldly saying that the God of the Old Testament is the God of Christian faith, one might more honestly say that people in ancient times put words into the mouth of God. This God—who presumably had an issue with violence and hatred—is often nothing more than the image and likeness of people over the centuries who were also filled with hatred, xenophobia, genocidal inclinations, and violence. The Bible traces the religious thought of ancient Israel. Such thought evolves, corrects itself, and eventually matures into beauty. While this evolution toward beauty may be seen within the Old Testament itself, it finds its fulfillment in the Gospels, in which Jesus teaches us to love our enemies, to turn the other cheek, to pray for those who hurt us, and to forgive those who wrong us from hearts of love.

While many examples might be given, I will here use the Ten Commandments to illustrate the evolutionary process within the

Bible. Particularly in the time of the Reformers, it was thought that the Ten Commandments contained in nutshell form a supreme and unchanging morality—which is why, for example, in his *Institutes of the Christian Religion* John Calvin could devote a whole section to a discussion of the Ten Commandments. But far from being eternally unchanging moral principles, the use and understanding of the Ten Commandments have been altered and understood in different ways through history. In the following paragraphs, I will discuss some features of the Ten Commandments that originally presupposed a very different context than our own.

To begin with, the Ten Commandments are to be seen in light of other collections of commandments in the ancient Near Eastern world—and there were many. Because of the geographical proximity of various societies, such societies shared common laws. The commonality of the laws was also a product of the general outlook and way of thinking that such societies had. One feature that many law-codes had in common was *lex talionis*, "eye for eye." Here is law #196 from the law-code of Hammurabi: "If a man destroys the eye of another man, they shall destroy his eye. If one breaks a man's bone, they shall break his bone." This "eye for eye" principle was central to most law codes, not only in a literal way but also in symbolic ways—for the part of the body that did the offending was maimed or severed: a hand might be cut off that struck a father, that a malpracticing surgeon used, or that a brander of a slave used; a breast might be cut off of a nursing woman who did not care for a child; a tongue might be cut off of a slanderer; an eye might be gouged out that looked into someone else's affairs; and a father's son might be killed if the father killed someone else's son. One cannot fail to see the correspondence between such "eye for eye" laws and Mosaic correspondences:

> If any harm follows, then you shall give life for life, eye for eye, tooth for tooth, hand for hand, foot for foot, burn for burn, wound for wound, stripe for stripe (Exod 21:23–25).

> Anyone who maims another shall suffer the same injury
> in return: fracture for fracture, eye for eye, tooth for
> tooth; the injury inflicted is the injury to be suffered (Lev
> 24:19–20).

> Show no pity: life for life, eye for eye, tooth for tooth,
> hand for hand, foot for foot (Deuteronomy 19:21).

Another correspondence between ancient Near Eastern thinking and the Ten Commandments may be seen in the first commandment: "you shall have no other gods before me." This commandment presupposes the existence of other gods. This accords with the religious evolution of primitive societies which often went from polytheism (the belief in many gods), to henotheism (the belief in many gods, but devotion only to one), to monotheism (the belief in one God). In pre-exilic times there was a conflict in Israel over the precise form of henotheism that the nation was going to embrace, such that much of the Old Testament assumes that foreign deities actually existed. The question was not one of existence, but one of devotion: "Given that it was Yahweh who called us out of Egypt, does it not follow that our allegiance should be solely to him, and not to other deities?"

The relative nature of the Ten Commandments is also seen in the different ways that they were transmitted. The following is but one example. In Exodus 20, the fourth commandment reads this way:

> Six days you shall labour and do all your work. But the
> seventh day is a sabbath to the LORD your God; you shall
> not do any work—you, your son or your daughter, your
> male or female slave, your livestock, or the alien resident
> in your towns. For in six days the LORD made heaven and
> earth, the sea, and all that is in them, but he rested on the
> seventh day; therefore the LORD blessed the sabbath day
> and consecrated it.

The rationale here given for keeping the sabbath day is that just as the Lord rested on the seventh day, so those who worship him should rest on the seventh day. This is very different from what we find in the recounting of the giving of the ten commandments in Deuteronomy 5, where the fourth commandment reads this way:

> Observe the sabbath day and keep it holy, as the LORD your God commanded you. Six days you shall labor and do all your work. But the seventh day is a sabbath to the LORD your God; you shall not do any work—you, or your son or your daughter, or your male or female slave, or your ox or your donkey, or any of your livestock, or the resident alien in your towns, so that your male and female slave may rest as well as you. Remember that you were a slave in the land of Egypt, and the LORD your God brought you out from there with a mighty hand and an outstretched arm; therefore the LORD your God commanded you to keep the sabbath day.

While some of the differences between the fourth commandment in Exodus and Deuteronomy only amount to particular wording, what is particularly striking is the rationale for the commandment. Whereas the rationale in Exodus is to mirror the original creation week, in Deuteronomy the rationale given is the Egypt experience: the people were to recall that they, too, were once slaves, so they should not force their slaves to work on the sabbath day. The different rationales for keeping the sabbath day may be explained on the basis of the overall concerns of the respective editors: whereas the editor of Exodus 20 may have had priestly matters at the forefront of his mind (part of which was concern with the liturgical calendar), the editor of Deuteronomy 5 was more concerned with history—in which deliverance from Egypt provides the paradigm for all acts of salvation.

Far from providing a supreme, unchanging, morality, at an early stage the Ten Commandments were thus adapted to suit various concerns. As centuries passed, however, the tendency to absolutize the commandments became unstoppable. The principal reason for this was the canonization of the Torah, the first five books of the Bible ("canonization" refers to the process in which a community of faith comes to the conclusion that literature that had hitherto only been religiously authoritative becomes fixed as

Scripture). Once the Torah had become canonized, not a word or a letter of it could be adjusted; and because the Ten Commandments are part of the Torah, it follows that they, too, could not be changed. I noted above how John Calvin absolutized the Ten Commandments. Such absolutization has also existed in Judaism. In the mind of some, the Ten Commandments are eternal. As such, they pre-existed creation. I think of the (rather humorous) legendary dispute between the letters of the Hebrew alphabet in Jewish lore: *Alef* (the first letter of the Hebrew alphabet) complained that it, rather than *Bet* (the second letter of the Hebrew alphabet), ought to have begun the Bible. *Alef* was consoled when it was told that it began the Ten Commandments ("I" of "I am the LORD your God . . ." begins with the letter *Alef*). Contrary to traditional convictions both in Judaism and Christianity, an analysis of the Ten Commandments shows that they underwent great change through the centuries.

The Ten Commandments nicely fit into the emphasis that Jesus placed on love. The first four commandments concern love for God, while the latter six commandments concern love for neighbor. When Jesus said that the greatest commandment is to love God with everything (thereby mirroring the first four commandments), and the second greatest commandment is to love one's neighbor (thereby mirroring the latter six commandments), Jesus was being consistent with the literary structure of the Ten Commandments. But the two great commandments of Jesus, which are a summary of the ten, may themselves be understood as one: love for God necessarily finds its fulfillment in love for others, such that the two loves cannot be separated or even distinguished. The author of 1 John suggests as much:

> We know love by this, that he laid down his life for us—and we ought to lay down our lives for one another. How does God's love abide in anyone who has the world's goods and sees a brother or sister in need and yet refuses help? Little children, let us love, not in word or speech, but in truth and action. . . . Whoever does not love does not know God, for God is love. God's love was revealed

among us in this way: God sent his only Son into the world so that we might live through him. In this is love, not that we loved God but that he loved us and sent his Son to be the atoning sacrifice for our sins. Beloved, since God loved us so much, we also ought to love one another. No one has ever seen God; but if we love one another, God lives in us, and his love is perfected in us. . . . Those who say, "I love God," and hate their brothers or sisters, are liars; for those who do not love a brother or sister whom they have seen, cannot love God whom they have not seen. The commandment we have from him is this: those who love God must also love their brothers and sisters (1 John 3:16–18; 4:8–12, 20–21).

There is a great pre-history to the Ten Commandments. Such commandments were themselves changed as believers adapted them to suit different contexts. The commandments were eventually absolutized, but even after they became scripture, Jesus interpreted them through the lens of love—two loves that eventually became thought of as one love.

The evolutionary nature of the commandments may also be seen in the Gospels. Matthew, in particular, goes to great lengths to show that the teaching of Jesus is an upgrade of the teaching of Moses (especially with regard to the "eye for eye" teaching). Matthew suggests that, with Jesus, a new Moses has come on the scene. Whereas the first Moses fled from oppression in Egypt to Canaan, the second Moses, Jesus, fled from oppression in "Canaan" (that is, Judea) to Egypt. This reversal is furthered in the Sermon on the Mount—for in five instances in his sermon, Jesus quoted Moses only to challenge him.

You have heard that it was said to those of ancient times, "You shall not murder"; and "whoever murders shall be liable to judgment." But I say to you . . . (Matt 5:21–22)

You have heard that it was said, "You shall not commit adultery." But I say to you . . . (Matt 5:27–28)

You have heard that it was said to those of ancient times,
"You shall not swear falsely, but carry out the vows
you have made to the Lord." But I say to you . . . (Matt
5:33–34)

You have heard that it was said, "An eye for an eye and
a tooth for a tooth." But I say to you . . . (Matt 5:38–39)

You have heard that it was said, "You shall love your
neighbour and hate your enemy." But I say to you . . .
(Matt 5:43)

The common thread in each challenge is that whereas the
teaching of Moses only concerned the outward and the physical,
Jesus applied the commandment to the inward and the spiritual—
it is not enough to be outwardly obedient, for one's heart must be
changed. Significant for our purposes, Jesus quoted two of the Ten
Commandments: one who hates another has already committed
murder, even as one who lusts after another has already committed
adultery. Those who follow Jesus are not simply to be concerned
with their behavior, for they are to be forever wary of the condition
of their hearts—Jesus is concerned with the transformation of the
heart, not with the modification of one's behavior. Also significant
is the fact that Jesus quoted an "eye for eye" verse in Moses—but
rather than repaying violence with violence, the disciple of Jesus is
to repay violence with love.

The "But I say to you . . ." teachings in the Sermon on the
Mount undermine every attempt (and the attempts through history are legion) to absolutize the commandments, for such teachings assume change. Israel, and then with it, the church and all
humanity steadily progress toward goodness—such that what was
condoned in the past becomes anathema in the present. Such development is just what one might expect, for when we look at our
own lives we can trace development toward goodness. The individual is a microcosm of all humanity—for like the individual, all
humanity is on a track toward goodness. The Scriptures are also on
this track: one can trace within them a progression from outward

obedience to interior transformation, from violence and hatred to peace and love. Together with all humanity, the Scriptures are forever changing and adapting.

Make no mistake. The Bible is a life-giving book from God. I have not sought to disparage it, only to rescue it from the abuses of fallen humanity—a humanity that feels the need for a book. I have also sought to rescue the Bible from religious authorities within fallen humanity who do back-flips to ensure that people interpret and understand this book in their way. I adore Scripture. Scripture holds up a mirror to me (the same fallenness within Scripture is within me, even as the evolutionary history that Scripture underwent is akin to the evolution of my own journey). Scripture helps me to understand mercy. Scripture reinforces to me that I must trust in God, not myself or this broken world. Scripture gives me hope for a better tomorrow—a hope that shapes the present even as it defines the future. I say a resounding Yes to Scripture. But what are my reasons for such a Yes? My affirmation has nothing to do with defining the objective authority of Scripture, for in my mind the Scriptures find their authority in the subjective world—the world of convictions, aspirations, hopes, desires, and devotion. While the authority of the Bible may well have an objective basis, all attempts through history to find and define such a basis have failed—they are all alike painfully unpersuasive. As history has repeatedly shown, all attempts at situating the authority of Scripture in science, history, or philosophy (i.e., outside the human heart) have only led to ugliness. The authority of Scripture is seen in how it compels the believer to be like Jesus. Such authority must not be sought after in its historicity, inner consistency, or philosophical integrity. Scripture is not to be affirmed because it is consistent with what the world thinks it must look like. Scripture is to be affirmed because it compels one to be a better Christian, even as it reminds one to love God and neighbor.

Intertwined within the Old Testament there is both ugliness and beauty. This ugliness, that is counter to the love of God in Jesus, makes itself known as the Scriptures unravel what it means to be ideally human. But the beauty shines through the ugliness, for in the ugliness we see mercy at every turn. Every patriarch, for example, is depicted as selfish, but Joseph was right when he said to his brothers, "You meant it for evil, but God meant it for good" (Gen 50:20). Again, most every character in Judges is flawed and creates ugliness, but God works his beauty through such ugliness. Such beauty working through ugliness is especially seen in how God restores humanity to himself through the servant in Isaiah. This servant is mistreated horribly: people pluck out the hairs of his beard, they beat him, they spit on him, they insult him, and they regard him as a failure. But in spite of, and only through such ugliness, God again creates his beauty—for through the despised servant, humanity is restored and accepts the mercy of God. The beauty that only comes from the ashes of ugliness is equally present in the New Testament, for its central story is about how the beauty of God was present even in the ugliest of human injustices—"God was in Christ, reconciling the world to himself" (2 Cor 5:19). The Bible likewise enjoins the believer to be an instrument of beauty when faced with the ugliness of the world. The believer is to repay hatred with love, the believer is to forgive completely and unconditionally, the believer is to see the best in every person, and the believer must strive for peace. Insofar as the church becomes entangled in worldly disputes about the nature of Scripture, it only furthers the story of ugliness—even as it fails to be an instrument of beauty.

4

Heretical Orthodoxy

What has the concern with orthodoxy produced in the world? If we judged orthodoxy by the fruit that it produced, we would condemn it—for Jesus taught that "you will know them by their fruits" (Matt 7:16). So-called Christian kings and bishops who sanctioned the killing or enslavement of Jews, Muslims, and pagans is well documented. Such animosity did not limit itself to the killing of unbelievers, for orthodoxy was just as merciless to those within the ranks of Christendom. One can think of the way that Bishop Augustine sanctioned the killing of the Donatists, how Athanasius sought to obliterate the Arian heresy by any means, and how, centuries later, the Protestants killed one another—even as the Roman Catholic Church slaughtered heretics in the Inquisition.

All the same, the argument that Christian faith has caused violence is wrongheaded—for it was not Christian faith that committed such atrocities, but the universal human tendency to despise anyone who thinks and lives differently. Societies have always despised what they have failed to understand. This is true of the ideological violence that the twentieth century witnessed, little of which had to do with religion: communists killed capitalists, despot overthrew tyrant, bloody coups toppled hated regimes, and democracies justified violence because they were fighting for freedom. Joseph Stalin killed twelve million possible dissenters, Adolf Hitler obliterated six million Jews, Pol Pot wiped out scores in Cambodia, Mao Tse Tung killed some forty million in China, Idi Amin was ruthless to dissenters in Uganda, even as the cold-war between America and the Soviet Union ravaged the world. This list could go on and on. Even today's Islamic terrorists are not violent for religious reasons. They say they are, but it is not true. Their religion is but an instrument of the hatred that is within their hearts. Religion gives them voice and justifies their violence. It is not religion that has led to violence, but the universal preoccupation with self that says, "I am right, you are wrong." Like all people, the terrorists want power, they hate to be mistreated, and they use religion to justify the violence that they use. True and life-giving religion abhors such mentality.

The violence that has been perpetrated in the name of Jesus has similarly been justified by one Christian sect or another with the assertion that "others are wrong and we are right"—and God presumably hates wrong thinking. This assertion is akin to the ethnocentrism of humanity—the individual evaluates every society through the lens of their own culture. I witnessed such ethnocentrism when I lived in Africa, for some of the Christian missionaries whom I worked with were more concerned that the Africans did things the American way than they were with the Africans embracing the kingdom. Such missionaries were hopelessly unable to distinguish between their societal values and the gospel, a gospel that humbly embraces different perspectives in every society. I have also witnessed such ethnocentrism in China, where some Western Christians have unreflectively sought to transplant their Western Christian faith into the East. Rather than trying to understand different cultures, well-meaning Christians have imposed their understanding of the gospel upon others—but the gospel transcends cultural norms. The assertion that "others are wrong and we are right" leads, more menacingly, to xenophobia—fear and hatred of other cultures. Such fear is based on ignorance, for we fear what we do not understand. This assertion lacks the humility that is the basis of Christian faith. When we are truly humble, we recognize that all that is good within us comes from

God—even as we recognize God-given beauty within every society (however godless it might be) and every individual (however disagreeable they might be).

The violence that is intrinsic to "I am right and you are wrong" thinking has expressed itself throughout human history in countless ways. From the quarrelling of couples to societal squabbling to geopolitical strife, the arrogance of "I am right and you are wrong" thinking has been a foundation stone of all human relationships. With respect to Christian faith, this assertion has led to the divide between orthodox and heretical belief. Orthodox belief is belief that has variously been defined as that which is consistent with "what the New Testament teaches," with "what the apostles taught," with "the ongoing tradition of the universal church" (or an amalgamation of such things). Heretical belief does not, typically, disregard any of the above. Heretical belief, rather, often reinterprets the above: even as it says belief must be consistent with the historic faith, it says that standard interpretations of the historic faith are wrong. Heresy itself inevitably becomes orthodoxy. Whereas splinter groups initially seek to distance themselves from the main group, they themselves become the lens through which truth must be understood—such that they set themselves up as the standard of true belief. What usually happens is that splinter groups become the main group, and splinters of splinters necessarily arise. Orthodox belief is tied to such splintering—even as it makes the assertion that it preserves the unchanging truth of the New Testament, the apostolic teaching, or the tradition of the universal church. Orthodoxy is thus based on heresy.

Christianity itself started as a heresy of a splinter group within Judaism—Pharisaic Judaism. This group within Judaism became the dominant group for it focused on the Hebrew Bible—sacred literature that outlasted the temple, the monarchy, or the possession of land. The Pharisees outlasted any group that had political aspirations simply because they found their salvation in the Scriptures and not in anything that could be destroyed, overthrown, or seized—such as the temple, the monarchy, or the land. One sect of Pharisaic Judaism in the first century was the sect of

Christians—people who believed that Jesus of Nazareth was the messiah. The book of Acts tells us that "it was in Antioch that the disciples were first called Christians" (11:26). Prior to this, those who believed that Jesus of Nazareth was the promised messiah were thought of as belonging to "the Way" (e.g., Acts 9:2). It would have been unthinkable for such believers to think that they were not Jews, for in their mind "the Way" was the fulfillment of Judaism. Because Jewish thinking typically had no place in its thought for a crucified messiah, it regarded the Christian sect as an affront. But Christians taught that the crucifixion of the messiah was far from a defeat, for within it salvation was afforded. Christians also taught that following his crucifixion, this messiah rose from the dead—thereby ushering in the end of the world. Pharisaic Judaism felt threatened by the Christian sect, for this sect was becoming too populous and powerful. Sometime near the end of the first century, Pharisaic Judaism therefore distanced itself from the Christian sect. The separation was tragic for some, and perhaps a welcomed blessing to others. I am sure that the destruction of the Jewish temple was variously interpreted: some Jews might have said, "the reason why the Romans destroyed the temple is because God has punished us for the Jesus heresy"; and those sympathetic with the Jesus sect might have said "the reason why the Romans destroyed the temple is because God has shown that Christianity is the fulfillment of Judaism." Christianity thus began as a heresy; but like many heresies, the heresy of Christianity itself eventually became an orthodoxy—and many heresies arose from within its ranks.

In the early centuries of the church, various arguments concerning the nature of Jesus arose. Many questions concerned how Jesus was related to God. Two of the heresies had polar opposite viewpoints: while the Arians contended that Jesus was entirely human, the Docetists had the opposite view—Jesus only appeared to be human. The view that won (and became orthodox) was that Jesus was fully human and fully God at the same time, a view that was furthered in later trinitarian doctrine—God is Father, Son, and Holy Spirit. The criteria for decision-making consisted of the

Bible, the teaching of the apostles, and the tradition of the church. All such criteria were themselves the subject of debate: while the books of the Bible had essentially been decided upon, there was still room for debate; precisely what is apostolic was debated (e.g., was the teaching of the apostles' disciples apostolic?); and it is more accurate to speak of the traditions of the church, for there was no single tradition. Important for our purposes, though, is not which side was correct, but how it was concluded what was heretical and what was orthodox. There were no omens, earthquakes, or voices from heaven to help in the decision-making: the decision about divine truth was made as any other important decisions might be made—through a vote. Constantine, a Roman emperor of the fourth century, invited bishops throughout the empire to a council in Nicaea. The council met for more than two months. The issue regarding the relationship of Jesus to God was voted upon. To enforce the conclusions of the vote, the state became involved— and all dissenters were judged as heretics, but the matter was not over. Constantine's son, Constantinus, then became the emperor. Constantinus reversed the anti-Arian policy of his father—such that the orthodoxy of Nicaea became heretical, and anti-Arian bishops were persecuted and deposed. But after Constantinus, another reversal took place, and by the end of the fourth century the Nicene view became fixed. Orthodoxy was ultimately decided upon, and then enforced, by power. Machiavelli was correct: might makes right.

Trinitarian orthodoxy once again became an issue with the divide within Christianity in the eleventh century. Unlike previous controversies, however, the dispute was not between trinitarian and Arian teaching, but within trinitarian teaching itself. The debate focused on a single clause within the creed: did the Holy Spirit proceed from the Father, or from the Father "and the Son"? Orthodox Christians (Christians from the Eastern portion of the empire) opted for the former, while Roman Catholic Christians (Christians from the Western portion of the empire) opted for the latter. This doctrinal dispute raged even as a dispute about power raged: whereas Roman Catholic bishops wanted all of

Christendom to view the bishop of Rome as the leader of the faith, Orthodox bishops wanted all of Christendom to view the bishop of Constantinople as the leader of the faith. This argument was tied to the decline of the empire itself—during which power moved from the West to the East. (Forgive me. I have oversimplified the matter. The schism between the East and West also included the very important matters of when to celebrate Easter, and whether one should use leavened or unleavened bread in communion.) The doctrinal controversy was thus wed to the power controversy, and East and West both quickly anathematized each other (i.e., they both taught that one is not a true Christian if one believes in the other's heresy). The divide between Roman Catholicism and Orthodoxy remains to this day.

In the sixteenth century, the church in the West underwent a schism that, like the schism of the eleventh century, was based on doctrinal matters. One concern was over the place of the Bible in Christian faith. Was the Bible to be interpreted only in accordance with what the Roman Catholic church taught? Related to this question were questions regarding the authority of the church. Does the Roman Catholic Church have universal authority? Can individuals be Christians outside of the Roman Catholic Church? As with the schism of the eleventh century, such doctrinal concerns were tied to political matters. Princes in various parts of the empire did not like that Rome had jurisdiction over them. Such princes sided with those who opposed the Roman Church over doctrinal matters. This marriage between religion and politics was tremendously powerful—such that Protestantism was born. Protestants included any who dissented from Rome. The Church of Rome anathematized Protestants, even as Protestants referred to the Roman Church as the Anti-Christ, the great whore of Babylon, and many other less-than-kind appellatives. Wasting little time, Protestantism itself then divided between Lutherans, Calvinists, and Anabaptists. Such Protestants divided because they could not agree about baptism and communion: they fought and killed each other over whether such rites were sacraments or ordinances, and precisely how Christ is present at communion. Following the sixteenth century, there were many religious wars within Protestantism—even as the divides between Orthodoxy and Roman Catholicism, and Roman Catholicism and Protestantism, deepened. Splinter group came out of splinter group—each group saying that the other group is wrong and it is right. Like all human history, church history is "one damn thing after another." Church history is fraught with reckless selfishness, and it is comical in the extreme, but the comedy is dark—were it not so tragic, one could only laugh.

While it is true that there is nothing more heretical than merciless orthodoxy, there is, nevertheless, room for orthodoxy. The concern must not be the abandonment or elimination of orthodoxy, but the reshaping and conversion of it. To be in line with the true faith, orthodoxy must first recognize that it contributes to goodness only insofar as it leads to greater love for God and people. All true doctrine furthers one's understanding of the love of God in Jesus—whether it be any aspect of Christology, soteriology, ecclesiology, or eschatology. Orthodoxy must also become more generous (I here have in mind a book called *Generous Orthodoxy*): it must not make mountains out of mole hills; and it must strive to build up rather than tear down. I have known many Christians who, because they emphasized doctrine more than love, have become ineffectual, lifeless, and sullen. What is true of the individual is also true of churches. Those churches that emphasize that they are the best representations of God (because they deem themselves to be orthodox) tend to be the worst. (The most graceless churches are the ones that emphasize, in a rather grace-less way, that you must believe in their understanding of grace to be saved.) The conversion of orthodoxy would also be reflected in its humility. Orthodoxy would do well to reflect on Paul's teaching that "knowledge puffs up, but love builds up" (1 Cor 8:1). Orthodoxy must remember that Jesus thanked his Father for hiding truth "from the wise and the intelligent" and revealing it "to infants" (Matt 11:25). The conversion of orthodoxy assumes its self-crucifixion, but orthodoxy takes itself way too seriously to crucify itself—as if the cosmos itself was at stake. Orthodoxy is far too concerned with maintaining power. As such, it does not reflect on the Savior's teaching, "Woe to you when all speak well of you, for that is what their ancestors did to the false prophets" (Luke 6:26). Orthodoxy does not remember that Jesus himself was a heretic, and that Jesus loved heretics and all who were outside Israel—even as he accused the religious establishment with hypocrisy.

As room needs to be made for orthodoxy, so there must also be room for heterodoxy. Heresy forces the church to formulate its belief systems; and were it not for heresy, orthodoxy would not exist. I noted above that one criterion that the church used in defining orthodoxy was the Bible. I also noted that the Bible was itself subject to discussion because the church had not come to a definite conclusion regarding what books to include or exclude. The heretic Marcion forced the church to come to a decision. Marcion taught that the god of the Old Testament was not the God of the New Testament. Because the god of the Old Testament was altogether different from the God and Father of Jesus, the god of the Old Testament was to have nothing to do with Christian faith. The Old Testament was thus to be cast aside, as were those parts of the New Testament that were deeply indebted to the Old Testament. Marcion's Bible consisted of eleven books: portions of Luke and ten writings attributed to Paul—all of which were altered by Marcion to make them consistent with his own teachings. The early church denounced Marcion's teachings as being heretical; but as a consequence of Marcion's heresy, the church was compelled to provide a list of the books of the Bible. While this list was not finalized, and while many questions regarding different books remained, Marcion had forced the church to make a decision. Heresy was thus the impetus of orthodoxy.

Even as the disciple must strive to see goodness in all people, the disciple must strive to see goodness in heresy—for at the root of heresy there is often a concern with something that orthodoxy has overlooked or underemphasized. At the root of the Marcionite heresy is the contention that there is discontinuity between the depiction of God in the Old Testament and the depiction of God in the New Testament. To solve such tension, early Christians proposed different models of interpretation. Many Christians used one or another method of allegorization, in which different levels of meaning were applied to every text—such that the Old Testament was spiritualized: Jerusalem might be heaven, killing others might be violence against personal sin, the ark of Noah might be the womb of Mary through which the world was delivered, etc. Such views were themselves based on earlier views: implicit to Jesus' statement that "Moses said . . . , but I say . . ." is the belief in discontinuity, even as Paul's contention that Christ is the goal of the Hebrew Bible also assumes discontinuity. The difference, though, between early Christian interpretation of the Old Testament and the Marcionite heresy is that whereas early Christians saw continuity within discontinuity, Marcion saw no continuity whatsoever.

The felt need for orthodoxy can be seen in the knowing-doing-being triad. The three aspects of the triad are interrelated: knowing influences doing, even as doing then shapes being, and so on. In the world of religion, knowing is tied to doctrine and orthodoxy, doing is practicing goodness, and being is having one's heart transformed. The saints of orthodoxy are not humble servants, but towering intellects—an Augustine, an Aquinas, a Luther, a Calvin. Just as knowledge uses power to coerce others to accept it, and to condemn those who do not, orthodoxy uses power to bring others in line—and each of the above-mentioned saints of orthodoxy used force and violence. When it has had the wherewithal to do so, orthodoxy has used the power of the state—compelling heretics and unbelievers to accept its teaching on pain of death, imprisonment, or exile. When orthodoxy has not had the backing of the state, it has used the argument that to differ with it is to invite eternal damnation—for God loathes heretics. When orthodoxy knows that it cannot play this card, it uses the socialization card: those who do not think the way that their community thinks are in danger of being rejected. (The message is the same—whether it be the excommunication of Roman Catholicism, the shunning of the Jehovah's Witnesses, the disfellowshipping of the Baptists, or the simple non-membership of other groups.) Orthodoxy must ask itself why it prizes knowledge above doing and being.

The philosopher Søren Kierkegaard had a great problem with the Lutheran orthodoxy of nineteenth-century Denmark. Kierkegaard rightly abhorred all orthodoxy that did not produce life. In one of his parables, Kierkegaard likened many theologians to architects, draftsmen, and interior decorators of a great mansion. Such people carefully described and defined the mansion—its high ceilings, stately rooms, oak rails, marble floors, bronze door handles, and the like. The tragic thing is that rather than living amidst such luxury, these people chose to live in the cellar! When Christians focus on knowing, on an orthodoxy that is not wed to life, they likewise live in the basement. Not unlike Kierkegaard, Dietrich Bonhoeffer challenged the Lutheranism of early twentieth-century Germany. In his influential *Cost of Discipleship*, Bonhoeffer spoke of "cheap grace"—an understanding of grace that has few ramifications for how the Christian is actually to live. Such cheap grace says to the disciple, "you have been baptized," or "you have gone to confession," or "you have participated in the eucharist," or "you have been born again," and "you are therefore in God's graces." Such thinking, which the church enables, is rampant in today's Christianity—even as it was in Bonhoeffer's day.

Orthodoxy is correct, though. There is a place for violence. But such violence is not to be directed at others—to those who compromise the truth of the gospel, to heretics, or to unbelievers. The only violence that can be justified is the violence of love. I here think of Jesus's "violence" saying:

> From the days of John the Baptist until now the kingdom of heaven has suffered violence, and the violent take it by force (Matt 11:12).

Much ink has been spilt over the meaning of this saying—often because it does not seem to be in accord with the common understanding of a meek and mild Jesus. The verb *biazomai* (to force, dominate), its equivalent noun *biastēs* (a violent person), and the verb *harpazō* (to seize) are often softened so that the saying sounds less harsh. But such softening is illegitimate. The saying needs to be understood in light of other harsh and violent sayings of Jesus.

If your right eye causes you to sin, gouge it out and throw it away; it is better for you to lose one of your members than for your whole body to be thrown into hell. And if your right hand causes you to sin, cut it off and throw it away; it is better for you to lose one of your members than for your whole body to go into hell. (Matt 5:29–30)

Do not think that I have come to bring peace to the earth; I have not come to bring peace, but a sword. For I have come to set a man against his father, and a daughter against her mother, and a daughter-in-law against her mother-in-law; and one's foes will be members of one's own household. Whoever loves father or mother more than me is not worthy of me; and whoever loves son or daughter more than me is not worthy of me; and whoever does not take up the cross and follow me is not worthy of me. Those who find their life will lose it, and those who lose their life for my sake will find it. (Matt 10:34–39).

To another he said, "Follow me." But he said, "Lord, first let me go and bury my father." But Jesus said to him, "Let the dead bury their own dead; but as for you, go and proclaim the kingdom of God." Another said, "I will follow you, Lord; but let me first say farewell to those at my home." Jesus said to him, "No one who puts a hand to the plow and looks back is fit for the kingdom of God." (Luke 9:59–62).

People violently taking the kingdom by force is entirely congruent with the above teachings of Jesus. Such people are those who are consumed by Jesus and his message. This is the "violence of love" of which Oscar Romero spoke.

We have never preached violence, except the violence of love, which left Christ nailed to a cross, the violence that we must each do to ourselves to overcome our selfishness and such cruel inequalities among us. The violence we preach is not the violence of the sword, the violence of hatred. It is the violence of love, of brotherhood, the violence that wills to beat weapons into sickles for work.[1]

1. Romero, *Violence*, 25.

One of the greatest impediments to the violence of love has ironically come from the church itself as it has focused on orthodoxy. In the modern world, orthodoxy concerns itself with the sacraments, with conversion, or with "making a decision to have a personal relationship with Jesus"—being "born again." A very real problem that comes with such perspectives is the assumption that growing into the image of God is not paramount: most important, so it is thought, is whether one is in covenant with God or if one has been saved. Such mind-sets are counter to what one finds throughout the New Testament, which stresses that the necessary outworking of "being in covenant" or "being saved" is growth in love for God and people. Where such growth is negligible (or even absent), there one is confronted with empty religion. The words of John the Baptist are here on the mark:

> Do not presume to say to yourselves, "We have Abraham as our ancestor"; for I tell you, God is able from these stones to raise up children to Abraham. Even now the ax is lying at the root of the trees; every tree therefore that does not bear good fruit is cut down and thrown into the fire. (Matt 3:9–10)

Contrary to cheap grace, the individual who strives to grow into the likeness of Jesus gives attention to this or that sacrament or this or that decision only insofar as doing so propels them further into the kingdom. Such people long for growth in Jesus as the desert wanderer pines for but a drop of water on his parched tongue. Here we see a passion that is greater than the addict's longing for a fix, a longing that church societies fail to appreciate, a passion that defies all categorizations—even as such passion may be ridden with angst. I am here reminded of that woman in the Gospel story who expressed undying love for Jesus as she wept, anointed Jesus' feet with oil, kissed his feet, and wiped them with her hair. Simon the Pharisee had great disregard for Jesus because Jesus seemingly failed to recognize that the woman was a "sinner."

> Then turning toward the woman, Jesus said to Simon, "Do you see this woman? I entered your house; you gave me no water for my feet, but she has bathed my feet with

her tears and dried them with her hair. You gave me no kiss, but from the time I came in she has not stopped kissing my feet. You did not anoint my head with oil, but she has anointed my feet with ointment. Therefore, I tell you, her sins, which were many, have been forgiven; hence she has shown great love. But the one to whom little is forgiven, loves little." (Luke 7:44–47)

The church has little room for socially unacceptable displays of affection for Jesus—be they charged with longings for mercy, for healing, or acceptance. Growing in the kingdom is not about being orthodox or becoming socially acceptable. Growing in the kingdom is all about falling headlong in passion for the truth of Jesus and his kingdom. The measure of success has nothing to do with worldly acclaim or disregard, but on crucifixion of the ego in order that more room may be given to the working of the Spirit.

Often lurking at the heels of orthodoxy is resistance to change, but salvation is a process—and not a static matter as orthodoxy seems to suggest, nor should salvation be dichotomized between the saved and the unsaved. The New Testament everywhere assumes that salvation is a process—from Jesus' parables to the many lists of virtues in the epistles. Paul's letter to the Philippians is explicit on this point: "work out your own salvation with fear and trembling" (Phil 2:12). In the same letter Paul could say, "I am confident of this, that the one who began a good work among you will bring it to completion by the day of Jesus Christ" (Phil 1:6), even as he told the Thessalonians that "we ought always to thank God for you, brothers, and rightly so, because your faith is growing more and more, and the love every one of you has for each other is increasing" (2 Thess 1:3). I here think of John Bunyan's classic *Pilgrim's Progress*. This work, which is a must-read from the seventeenth century, is an allegory in which Christian leaves City of Destruction to get to Celestial City. The many challenges that Christian meets on his way to Celestial City are personified in such antagonists as Obstinate, Pliable, Mr. Worldly Wiseman, Talkative, Mr. Legality, and Presumption—even as Christian journeys through such places as Valley of Despair, Slough of Despond,

Vanity Fair, Valley of the Shadow of Death, and Doubting Castle. Implicit to the allegory is that salvation is a process: while salvation can be tasted in this life, its fullness can only be known as the believer works through a host of obstacles that challenge it: between City of Destruction and Celestial City lies a plethora of characters and places that seek to dissuade Christian from progress.

Resistance to change is often based on pride—for change may well presuppose that we have been wrong, and to admit that one has been wrong requires humility. One problem that I have with heresy is not so much the opinion that it might have, but the attitude that upholds the opinion—for the attitude of pride sustains heresy. But this is not to say that orthodoxy excels in the virtue of humility where heresy has failed. Not at all. Pride in orthodoxy might be even greater than pride in heresy. One can be dead right, but dead all the same—and insofar as one is not open to change, one is spiritually dead.

Consistent with its dogged resistance to change, orthodoxy tends toward repristination: at the same time that orthodoxy concludes that its understanding of truth is beyond challenge, it often fixates on one era or another, or one one thinker or another—for in its mind such eras or thinkers had come to an unsurpassable understanding of truth. One sees such repristination wherever one sees a concern with orthodoxy. Such repristination is seen within the Roman Catholic tradition when the assertion is made that the mass should not be said in the common tongue, or when one saint or teacher is followed at the expense of others. Within the Protestant stream, some similarly assert that because the Reformers were so right, disciples of Jesus must follow Calvin, Luther, or Zwingli; even as some Anglicans look to the divines of the Oxford movement (who themselves sought to repristinate the faith). The list is endless, for all of orthodoxy seeks to follow and uphold its pioneers or founders. But faith knows little of repristination. The philosopher Jean-Paul Sartre rightly referred to this as "bad faith": repristinated faith is bad faith or disingenuous because it bases its faith on the thinking and experience of someone else. It thinks that "because this historic person had it right, and because I concur with this person in every way, I am also right." For faith to be good and true, it must be individualized. While famous thinkers of the past may well have had an uncommon grasp of the truth, their grasp can at best be a pointer for later people. Famous thinkers of the past might cry out from the grave, "I found truth here"; but they never cry out, "find the truth in the precise manner that I did"—for the dead know that every story is different.

In his *The Structure of Scientific Revolutions*, Thomas Kuhn discussed change with respect to the history of science. Kuhn contended that when a monumental shift in thought takes place such that one theory is replaced with another, all data that had been interpreted through the lens of the first theory must be reinterpreted through the lens of the new theory. Kuhn referred to this as a "paradigm shift." An example concerns the Copernican Revolution. Prior to Copernicus, scientific data was interpreted through the Ptolemaic theory that the sun orbited the earth. When, in the sixteenth century, the Copernican view overthrew the Ptolemaic theory, a paradigm shift of thought ensued in which all scientific data pertaining to the solar system had to be reinterpreted. Akin to Kuhn's idea, growth in the kingdom may well include one or more paradigm shifts—for the seeker of God is compelled to reinterpret their understanding of doctrinal matters as they become increasingly aware that various elements of their belief system are problematic.

Over the years I have gone through several paradigm shifts in my understanding of Christian faith. One such shift pertained to the nature of Scripture. Because at an earlier stage I believed that the Bible was a perfect mirror of the truth of God, I sought to have a thoroughgoing comprehension of the Bible—such that I memorized vast portions of the New Testament: all of Romans, Philippians, Hebrews, James, 1 Peter, and 1 John, together with many other sections of the Bible. It is not, moreover, that I just memorized such portions. I also had a rigorous routine in which I went over what I had memorized. If I missed a single conjunction I would go over the material again and again until I had it perfectly. My devotion to the Bible began to unwind, however,

when I started to study the historical processes that led to the creation and transmission of the Bible. At the undergraduate level of
my formal theological education, the subject of the formation of
the Bible never surfaced: it was always simply assumed that the
Bible was God-given—and this assumption was never subjected to
evaluation. At the graduate level, I was gently introduced to matters pertaining to the historical shaping of the Bible. I began to
rethink some of the categories of thought that I had received. At
the post-graduate level no holds were barred; and rather than being given only a biased understanding of the formation of the Bible
(an understanding that was as naive as it was well-meaning), I was
thrust into a world where I was learning about the formation of
the Bible—even as I painstakingly analyzed various portions of the
Bible in their original languages, in different manuscripts, and in
light of the social, political, and religious environments in which
such portions were written. Like almost all academics who studied
the Scriptures at this level, I eventually concluded that many of the
assumptions of conservative Protestantism concerning the nature
of Scripture were entirely indefensible. This created a most painful
paradigm shift in my spiritual development. All the same, it was
necessary for me to experience this paradigm shift, for doing so
has produced great life in me. As painful as it might have been,
I relish in the shift, but such relishing is only with 20/20 hind-
sight—at the time I would have preferred purgatory to the angst
that I was experiencing! Akin to how Copernicus and others may
have felt forlorn in the midst of the paradigm shift, so those who
seek God may go through painful seasons of doubt and social un-
rest. But those who seek God must remain steadfast, even as they
strive to rest in God amidst the pain. Spiritual paradigm shifts are
never the problem, for they are integral to the spiritual life; and
the humble reticently welcome paradigm shifts as they know that
though floodwaters of change may immerse them, God will keep
them in his care—even as they themselves mature in the faith.

5

Jesus, the Divine Loser

The title of this chapter will be offensive to many followers of Jesus. "How can Jesus be referred to as a loser? Was Jesus not the ideal human? Is it not blasphemous to speak of Jesus in this way?" Such questions may well be on the reader's mind, and rightly so—for it is not customary to think that Jesus was regarded as a loser. But I here say "regarded" and "loser" carefully, for everything about Jesus was thought to be substandard: his poverty, his religious ideas, his disinterest in politics, with whom he spent time, his relationships with family members, and the nature of his trial and execution. At best, Jesus was thought to be a misguided under-achiever; and at worst, Jesus was regarded as a dangerous heretic. But throughout history, followers of Jesus have too quickly aligned themselves with the divinity of Jesus. They have had little use or understanding of his humanity; and even when they try to understand his humanity they often get it wrong—for Jesus was not just any human, but the lowest of humans.

Before I write about how Jesus was thought to be a loser, I will discuss the background of the claim that Jesus was divine. The belief that the messiah would in some sense be divine finds its basis in the Old Testament. A good example is the identity of the angel of the Lord. In many instances in Genesis, the angel of the Lord seems to be identified with the Lord himself. The first example is in the story of Hagar. At first, it is the angel of the Lord who speaks to

Hagar—but a transition is made to it being the Lord himself who speaks to her.

> The angel of the LORD said to her, "Return to your mistress, and submit to her." The angel of the LORD also said to her, "I will so greatly multiply your offspring that they cannot be counted for multitude." And the angel of the LORD said to her, "Now you have conceived and shall bear a son; you shall call him Ishmael, for the LORD has given heed to your affliction. He shall be a wild ass of a man, with his hand against everyone, and everyone's hand against him; and he shall live at odds with all his kin." So she named the LORD who spoke to her, "You are El-roi"; for she said, "Have I really seen God and remained alive after seeing him?" (Gen 16:9–13)

Three times in these verses it is the angel of the Lord who spoke to Hagar, but at the end of this passage it is the Lord who spoke to her. The angel of the Lord has a similar role in the next story of Hagar.

> And God heard the voice of the boy; and the angel of God called to Hagar from heaven, and said to her, "What troubles you, Hagar? Do not be afraid; for God has heard the voice of the boy where he is. Come, lift up the boy and hold him fast with your hand, for I will make a great nation of him." (Gen 21:17–18)

If this seeming confusion between who is speaking (the angel of the Lord or the Lord?) happened only twice, one might easily explain it away (e.g., the words of the angel are one with the words of the Lord—even as one might say that the words of a law enforcement officer are one with the words of the law). But the fact that this intermingling happens many other times leads one to think otherwise: it happens in the story of the three visitors to Abraham in Genesis 18–19, near the ending of the story of Abraham's near-sacrifice of Isaac in Genesis 22, in the story of Jacob's dream at Bethel in Genesis 31, and in the blessing of Joseph by Jacob in Genesis 48:15–16. Outside of Genesis, this commingling of the Lord and the angel of the Lord appears in the story of the burning bush in Exodus 3, and in the story of Balaam in Numbers 22. Some may well have believed that this commingling of the Lord and the angel of the Lord suggests that the angel of the Lord somehow shared in divinity. An early source lends support to this interpretation, for this source states that "the name" of the Lord is in the angel of the Lord: "Be attentive to him and listen to his voice; do not rebel against him, for he will not pardon your transgression; *for my name is in him*" (Exod 23:21). This statement accords with what the angel of the Lord said to Samson's father Manoah: "Why do you ask my name? It is too wonderful" (Judg 13:17).[1]

Other verses that some Jews of Jesus' day might have used to show that the messiah would be divine include passages from later literature in the Old Testament. A passage in Daniel, which was often understood as referring to the messiah, suggests that the messiah would somehow be supra-human.

> As I watched in the night visions, I saw one like a son of man coming with the clouds of heaven. And he came to the Ancient One and was presented before him. To him was given dominion and glory and kingship, that all peoples, nations, and languages should serve him. His dominion is an everlasting dominion that shall not pass away, and his kingship is one that shall never be destroyed. (Dan 7:13–14)

Out of conviction that the messiah would be divine, many Jews of Jesus' day underscored the fact that the messiah would be worshipped. Perhaps more striking is a verse in Zechariah, which identifies an individual who would be "pierced" as being the Lord himself.

> And I will pour out a spirit of compassion and supplication on the house of David and the inhabitants of Jerusalem. They will look on *me* whom they have pierced, and they shall mourn for *him* as one mourns for an only child. (Zech 12:10)

---

1. That some early Christians understood the angel of the Lord in this way is intimated in Paul's teaching that the "spiritual rock" that accompanied the wandering Israelites was Christ himself (1 Cor 10:4).

Important for our purposes is the fact that the Lord here says that people will pierce "me," yet the same people would mourn for "him"—thereby suggesting that the "me" and the "him" are one and the same.[2] As with the other passages, this verse may well have been used as a basis for believing that the messiah would somehow be divine.

So then, within the Old Testament one may find reason to expect that the messiah would somehow be divine. Here it becomes very complicated, for many believed that the Old Testament also teaches that the messiah would be human—but not just any human, the lowest of humans, a slave and a loser. Limiting myself to the four "Servant Songs" of Isaiah, I will now discuss how some people in the time of Jesus believed that the messiah would be regarded as a loser. Here are the given passages.

> Here is my servant, whom I uphold, my chosen, in whom
> my soul delights; I have put my spirit upon him; he will
> bring forth justice to the nations. He will not cry or lift
> up his voice, or make it heard in the street; a bruised reed
> he will not break, and a dimly burning wick he will not
> quench; he will faithfully bring forth justice. He will not
> grow faint or be crushed until he has established justice
> in the earth; and the coastlands wait for his teaching. (Isa
> 42:1–4)

> Listen to me, O coastlands, pay attention, you peoples
> from far away! The LORD called me before I was born,
> while I was in my mother's womb he named me. He
> made my mouth like a sharp sword, in the shadow of
> his hand he hid me; he made me a polished arrow, in his
> quiver he hid me away. And he said to me, "You are my
> servant, Israel, in whom I will be glorified." But I said, "I
> have laboured in vain, I have spent my strength for noth-
> ing and vanity; yet surely my cause is with the LORD, and
> my reward with my God." And now the LORD says, who
> formed me in the womb to be his servant, to bring Jacob

---

2. Various translations seek to solve this grammatical problem by understanding "me" as "the one who"—but the grammatical problem is likely
intentional, and the Hebrew "me" is to be retained.

back to him, and that Israel might be gathered to him, for I am honoured in the sight of the LORD, and my God has become my strength—he says, 'It is too light a thing that you should be my servant to raise up the tribes of Jacob and to restore the survivors of Israel; I will give you as a light to the nations, that my salvation may reach to the end of the earth.' Thus says the LORD, the Redeemer of Israel and his Holy One, to one deeply despised, abhorred by the nations, the slave of rulers, "Kings shall see and stand up, princes, and they shall prostrate themselves, because of the Lord, who is faithful, the Holy One of Israel, who has chosen you." (Isa 49:1–7)

The Sovereign LORD has given me the tongue of a teacher, that I may know how to sustain the weary with a word. Morning by morning he wakens—wakens my ear to listen as those who are taught. The Sovereign LORD has opened my ear, and I was not rebellious, I did not turn backward. I gave my back to those who struck me, and my cheeks to those who pulled out the beard; I did not hide my face from insult and spitting. (Isa 50:4–6)

See, my servant shall prosper; he shall be exalted and lifted up, and shall be very high. Just as there were many who were astonished at him—so marred was his appearance, beyond human semblance, and his form beyond that of mortals—so he shall sprinkle many nations; kings shall shut their mouths because of him; for that which had not been told them they shall see, and that which they had not heard they shall contemplate. Who has believed what we have heard? And to whom has the arm of the LORD been revealed? For he grew up before him like a young plant, and like a root out of dry ground; he had no form or majesty that we should look at him, nothing in his appearance that we should desire him. He was despised and rejected by others; a man of suffering and acquainted with infirmity; and as one from whom others hide their faces he was despised, and we held him of no account. Surely he has borne our infirmities and carried our diseases; yet we accounted him stricken, struck down

by God, and afflicted. But he was wounded for our trans-
gressions, crushed for our iniquities; upon him was the
punishment that made us whole, and by his bruises we
are healed. All we like sheep have gone astray; we have all
turned to our own way, and the LORD has laid on him the
iniquity of us all. He was oppressed, and he was afflicted,
yet he did not open his mouth; like a lamb that is led to
the slaughter, and like a sheep that before its shearers is
silent, so he did not open his mouth. By a perversion of
justice he was taken away. Who could have imagined his
future? For he was cut off from the land of the living,
stricken for the transgression of my people. They made
his grave with the wicked and his tomb with the rich,
although he had done no violence, and there was no de-
ceit in his mouth. Yet it was the will of the LORD to crush
him with pain. When you make his life an offering for
sin, he shall see his offspring, and shall prolong his days;
through him the will of the LORD shall prosper. Out of
his anguish he shall see light; he shall find satisfaction
through his knowledge. The righteous one, my servant,
shall make many righteous, and he shall bear their iniquities. Therefore I will allot him a portion with the great,
and he shall divide the spoil with the strong; because he
poured out himself to death, and was numbered with
the transgressors; yet he bore the sin of many, and made
intercession for the transgressors. (Isa 52:13–53:12)

Far from bringing salvation to the world through worldly success, the messiah would bring salvation by becoming a suffering
and afflicted slave—even an abhorrent loser. The messiah would
have his "beard pulled out"; he would be a "slave," "struck," "spat
upon," "acquainted with infirmity," "rejected by others," "deeply
despised," "held of no account"; and he would be thought to be
"stricken" (by the Lord). As a result of such affliction, the messiah
would die ("he was cut off from the land of the living . . . they made
his grave with the wicked, and his tomb with the rich"), and live
again ("he shall prolong his days, and . . . out of his anguish he shall
see light"). That such affliction would eventually bring salvation

would astound everyone—even nations and kings "would shut their mouths because of him."

There are, thus, seemingly conflicting teachings within the Old Testament about the messiah: the messiah would somehow be divine, he would become dominant over his enemies—yet he would also suffer a great deal. It would take several centuries before the inner conflict of such teachings would be resolved. When we turn from the Old Testament to the New Testament, what we find is a progression of messianic thinking—a progression that may also be seen (albeit in different ways) in various Dead Sea scrolls.

The New Testament teaches that, yes, the messiah would be divine; and yes, this same messiah would also be the lowest of humans. While neither Matthew, nor Mark, nor Luke have anything explicit to say about the deity of Jesus, John comes close to stating that Jesus was God. (This should not surprise us, for John was one of the latest books of the New Testament to have been written.) Here are some passages in John that come close to stating that Jesus was God.

> The Father judges no one but has given all judgment to the Son, so that all may honour the Son just as they honour the Father (John 5:22–23).

This passage suggests that worship of Jesus must be the same as worship of the Father. According to John, some people believed that such language shows that Jesus thought that he was one with God:

> It is not for a good work that we are going to stone you, but for blasphemy, because you, though only a human being, are making yourself God (John 10:33).

Similar to this accusation is another:

> For this reason the Jews were seeking all the more to kill him, because he was not only breaking the sabbath, but was also calling God his own Father, thereby making himself equal to God (John 5:18).

Jesus never denied such accusations. The Jesus of John's Gospel, rather, would go on to say such remarkable things as "The Father and I are one" (John 10:30). But the Gospel of John stops short of stating the exact nature of the relationship between Jesus and God. This is nowhere more clear than in the very beginning of the Gospel of John, for while at the beginning of John we read that "the Word" was God, we do not there read that "Jesus" was God. No doubt, it is logical to conclude that because "the Word" became Jesus (see 1:14), Jesus was God—but John was not a slave to logic. Rather, John wanted his readers to embrace the mystery: yes, Jesus is one with God—but we must not demand to know precisely how. It is only different characters in John that could state that Jesus was one with God: we saw this above with the belief of the Jews; and what is true of the Jews was also true of Thomas. After his crucifixion, when Jesus appeared to the disciples, Thomas could say to him, "My Lord and my God!" (John 20:28). But Jesus himself never explicitly stated that he is one with God. While Jesus does not deny this, his words regarding his relationship to God are couched in ambiguity. This ambiguity is intentional. It is as if John did not want his readers to put Jesus in a box, to straitjacket him, to define him carefully so that the reader could control him.[3] Especially when it comes to religion, defining, straitjacketing, and controlling is paramount; but Jesus is beyond definition and control.

Indeed, parts of the New Testament teach that Jesus was one with God. While Christians have embraced this teaching, doing so has usually come at the expense of failing to see that parts of the New Testament also teach that Jesus was human, but not just any human—for as the lowest of humans, Jesus was regarded as a loser.

I recently had lunch with a kind and godly woman. As rich as her faith was, though, many of her concerns were doctrinal: she wanted to know exactly how I thought Jesus was one with God. I told her that what I believed about Jesus is the same as what the

---

3. This interpretation is consistent with the interpretation that states that Jesus chose the title "Son of Man" simply because there was no consensus about who the "Son of Man" might be. Stated otherwise, Jesus chose "Son of Man" for himself because he did not want people to have a definite (mis)understanding of who he was.

church has traditionally taught: Jesus is wholly God and wholly human at the same time. This did not satisfy her. She insisted that Jesus did not have any genes (for if he had genes, she was taught that it means that he inherited a sinful nature). In response I told her two things. First, the Bible says nothing on the matter. Second, stating that Jesus had no genes is denying that he was fully human. The woman's thoughts are typical, for many Christians today are uncomfortable with the humanity of Jesus. They do not like to think of Jesus as being hungry, tired, lonely, stressed, or unaware of the future. But such feelings are universal—one cannot be human without experiencing them. Like any human, Jesus needed to be alone to pray (e.g., Luke 5:16)—presumably because he needed to restore his energy. Like any human, Jesus could be physically exhausted and thirsty: in the story of the Samaritan woman, we read that Jesus was tired, and Jesus said to the woman "give me a drink" (John 4:6–7). Like any human, Jesus felt loneliness. Jesus could say, "Foxes have holes, and birds of the air have nests; but the Son of Man has nowhere to lay his head" (Matt 8:20). Jesus' heart-rending experience in the garden of Gethsemane is particularly telling of his humanity.

> In his anguish he prayed more earnestly, and his sweat became like great drops of blood falling down on the ground. When he got up from prayer, he came to the disciples and found them sleeping because of grief, and he said to them, "Why are you sleeping? Get up and pray that you may not come into the time of trial" (Luke 22:44–46).

We here find that, like many people facing stress, Jesus prayed earnestly. We also here read of the loneliness of Jesus, for like any human, he longed for company in his misery. The humanity of Jesus is likewise seen on the cross—especially when he cried out, "My God, my God, why have you forsaken me?" (Matt 27:46).

Well-meaning Christians often think that Jesus came out of the womb without any of the "weaknesses" of humanity. I here think of that famous Advent hymn "Away in a Manger," which includes "but little Lord Jesus, no crying he makes"—as if crying and fussing are sinful. It is as if even before he could crawl Jesus could say, "I am one with God . . . I have perfect knowledge . . . I am the second Person of the triune God." But no! Like any baby, Jesus needed to be changed and burped, he cried because he was too cold or too warm, or because he was hungry. Being a baby, Jesus needed human warmth: he needed to be comforted and held. The thinking that Jesus was beyond such frailty is contrary to what the Bible teaches. The following verse suggests as much: "Jesus increased in wisdom and in years, and in divine and human favour" (Luke 2:52).

The fact that Jesus "increased" in wisdom suggests that he developed mentally over the years: as time passed, Jesus was able to communicate in a wiser manner than when he was a child. Here is another verse: "About that day or hour no one knows, neither the angels in heaven, nor the Son, but only the Father" (Mark 13:32). Jesus himself did not know when he would return! Even as an adult, Jesus did not know all things. While there are many indications that Jesus had wondrous spiritual insight (e.g., the Gospels often say that "he knew what they were thinking"), far from being all-knowing, Jesus did not know some things.

At what point did Jesus become aware of his divine status? If Jesus developed mentally like any human being—if he grew in wisdom, if he did not know when he would return—at what point did he know that he was one with God? This is a question that has implications for how we understand what it is to follow Jesus. Some say that Jesus became aware of his divine status at his baptism, for at this time a voice from heaven said, "This is my Son, the Beloved, with whom I am well pleased" (Matt 3:17). Here we have three quotations from the Old Testament—each of which was thought to be about the messiah: "This is my Son" is from Psalm 2, "the Beloved" is from Genesis 22, and "with whom I am well pleased" is from Isaiah 45. Jesus might have known that God here announced that Jesus was the messiah—and that he was therefore somehow divine. Others have said that Jesus became aware of his divinity on the mount of transfiguration, where the voice from heaven said exactly the same thing as at his baptism (Matt 17:5). Others have said that while Jesus knew that he was the messiah, he did not know exactly what this meant. Perhaps Jesus knew that he was the messiah, and while he may have also known that he was somehow one with God, he did not know what all this entailed. I am only too aware that such speculation will make some angry, for I, too, once thought of Jesus as being only divine. I did not allow room for the humanity of Jesus. It is not that I was scared to do so. I thought that reading the Gospels in this way somehow compromised the truth of God in Jesus. But this interpretation does justice to the Gospel story, even as it helps us to understand the early believers' pondering of Jesus.

The early believers' understanding of Jesus' relationship with God may be seen in the *kenōsis* poem of Philippians 2, verses that have undergone much discussion through the millennia.

> Who, though he was in the form of God, did not regard equality with God as something to be exploited, but emptied himself, taking the form of a slave, being born in human likeness. And being found in human form, he humbled himself and became obedient to the point of death—even death on a cross. Therefore God also highly exalted him and gave him the name that is above every name, so that at the name of Jesus every knee should bend, in heaven and on earth and under the earth, and every tongue should confess that Jesus Christ is Lord, to the glory of God the Father. (Phil 2:6–11)

Many would say that this passage was written before Paul wrote Philippians, and that Paul inserted it here. Their conclusions are based on two observations: first, unlike the verses immediately before and after, this passage is lyrical or poetic in nature; and second, this passage includes language and ideas that are not found in other works of Paul. One can plausibly conclude from this poem that at least a segment of the early church believed that Jesus was one with God—for we here read that Jesus was "in the form of God," and he had "the name that is above every name." Furthermore, the poem states that "every knee should bend" and "every tongue should confess"—a quotation from Isaiah 45:23

that applies to Yahweh, the God of Israel. The conclusion is inescapable: even before Paul, very early in Christian thought, some Christians believed that Jesus was one with God. Also important for our purposes is the fact that this passage states that Jesus "emptied" himself. When the Word became flesh, when God became human in Jesus, he "emptied" himself. The question is, "of what did he empty himself"? Of what attribute did God empty himself when he became human? God is eternal (he never had a beginning and he will never have an end), immutable (unchanging), omnipresent (everywhere), omnipotent (all-powerful), and omniscient (all-knowing). Did God surrender one or more such attributes when he became human? The Christian tradition has answered this question with a resounding Yes. The reason that Jesus grew in wisdom and that he did not know when he would return is that when God became human in Jesus, he "emptied himself" of omniscience.

Jesus is the ideal human. He was crucified as a human for humanity; and he is the example for us to follow. We look to the story of Adam to see what we have been: obedient and then rebellious, innocent and then guilty, alive and then dead. Adam, a word which means "humanity," is not only an individual, for Adam represents every person who has ever lived. Adam is the prototype of all humanity. As such, what we see in Adam exists also in us—even as what exists in us existed first in Adam. Thankfully, however, a new Adam has come, Jesus of Nazareth. When we are followers of Jesus, when we take his teachings to heart, and when we become more like him, the old Adam slowly goes away and is replaced by this new Adam. Paul was possibly the first to make this connection between the two Adams.

> As all die in Adam, so all will be made alive in Christ. . . .
> Thus it is written, "The first man, Adam, became a living being"; the last Adam became a life-giving spirit. . . . The first man was from the earth, a man of dust; the second man is from heaven. As was the man of dust, so are those who are of the dust; and as is the man of heaven, so are those who are of heaven. Just as we have borne the image

of the man of dust, we will also bear the image of the man
of heaven (1 Cor 15:22, 45, 47–49).

Insofar as we follow Jesus, we cease to follow Adam. Followers of Jesus consist of a new humanity in which all things are
transformed. The humanity of Jesus has tremendous implications
for how the Christian must understand their life, for Jesus is the
example that the new humanity follows. We strive to give our
wealth away (not just to help others, but to help ourselves), we
must return love for hatred, we see beauty and hope where others
see ugliness and despair, we forgive even as we are forgiven, we desire simplicity rather than what is complex, we trust in God where
others only cling to what the world offers—and we recognize that
even while we will live for eternity, we are called in the here and
now to be instruments of the kingdom. We must know that the life
of Jesus is a model for our lives. Even as the story of Adam is our
story, we are to understand our lives through the story of Jesus. As
Jesus was humble, so we are to grow in humility—recognizing that
everything life-giving in us is from God. As Jesus cared for people,
so we are to have compassion on all—not just the "deserving" of
the world. As Jesus regarded his family as those who love God,
so our greatest human affections should be for those who want
God. As Jesus did not seek to make a name for himself, so we must
not strive for fame, fortune, or reputation. As Jesus did not love
God for what God could do for him, so we must seek God for
his face—not for his hands. And as Jesus remained silent during
his trial (before the religious authorities, Herod, and Pontius), so
we must not strive to defend ourselves (be it our reputation, the
respect that we think we deserve, how right we think we are, etc.).
Following Jesus must come from changed hearts. The vigilance
and commitment required for such change comes from within our
transformed selves, from our hearts. It is not enough to "do" what
is right, for as we are changed we "become" what is right. Doing
will necessarily come out of being: if we are filled with love, then
the goodness within us will certainly overflow into good deeds—
"By their fruits you will know them" (Matt 7:20). The Christian's
emphasis is on being. We look at our hearts and motivations with

great scrutiny, even as the Spirit replaces the old Adam with the new Adam. With all diligence, we "take every thought captive to obey Christ" (2 Cor 10:5). Such scrutiny is joyous and never somber, for we live by grace; and we know that his yoke is easy and his burden is light.

Let us return, then, to what the people might have expected of the messiah. All religious authorities thought that the messiah would be successful. Because Jesus was anything but successful, because he was regarded as a loser, people thought that he could not be the messiah. The messiah would, people believed, lead the nation to victory over its enemies. The messiah would be politically shrewd—even a conqueror, a military victor, the servant of God who would vanquish Rome. But who was this Jesus? Certainly not a conqueror. Jesus spoke of another kingdom—a kingdom that is beyond the tiny boundaries of political thought. Jesus never advocated hatred, militancy, or violence against Rome. Jesus was then crucified—a complete undermining of what the messiah was to be. A crucified messiah is a contradiction in terms, an oxymoron: the messiah would not suffer and die at the hands of men, but would destroy all the enemies of the nation. Paul could say the following of this contradiction: "We proclaim Christ crucified, a stumbling block to Jews and foolishness to gentiles" (1 Cor 1:22). Jesus was a stumbling block to the religious authorities because he was crucified—despised and unsuccessful before people, and accursed by God (for, according to Deuteronomy 21:23, anyone who was crucified was cursed by God). Even as the religious authorities of Jesus' day had no room in their thinking for a crucified messiah, so few followers of Jesus today have room in their thinking for understanding Jesus to be the lowest of humans. The reasoning goes something like this: "Yes, Jesus may have been human at some level, but he was a successful human all the same—and he wants me to be successful."

That Jesus was regarded as a loser is also clear from his life. The birth of Jesus was as unimpressive as was his death—born into a peasant family, serving rather than being served, and then executed as a criminal. That Jesus wanted his followers also to take the lowest position is clear from his teachings: he repeatedly taught that "the first will be last," that "those who exalt themselves will be humbled," and that "the greatest among you will be your servant."

> Many who are first will be last, and the last will be first (e.g., Matt 19:30).

> All who exalt themselves will be humbled, and all who humble themselves will be exalted (e.g., Matt 23:12).

> The greatest among you will be your servant (e.g., Matt 23:11).

> The least among all of you is the greatest (Luke 9:48).

> The greatest among you must become like the youngest, and the leader like one who serves (Luke 22:26).

That Jesus himself lived as a slave is clear from his actions—particularly when he washed his disciples' feet.

> So if I, your lord and teacher, have washed your feet, you also ought to wash one another's feet. For I have set you an example, that you also should do as I have done to you. (John 13:15–16)

Jesus here modelled slavery for his followers (only slaves would wash the feet of others). Like their master, the follower of Jesus must also serve others. The "ransom passage" likewise shows how Jesus both taught and lived servanthood.

> Whoever wishes to become great among you must be your servant, and whoever wishes to be first among you must be slave of all. For the Son of Man came not to be served but to serve, and to give his life a ransom for many. (Mark 10:43–45)

New Testament writings similarly emphasize that followers of Jesus must be slaves of others. For example, Paul tells his readers to "regard others as better than" oneself, and to have the same attitude of Jesus "who was in the form of a slave" (Phil 2:7).

Indeed, Jesus was regarded as a loser—but Jesus was a happy loser. The author of Hebrews could say the following.

> Therefore, since we are surrounded by so great a cloud of witnesses, let us also lay aside every weight and the sin that clings so closely, and let us run with perseverance the race that is set before us, looking to Jesus the pioneer and perfecter of our faith, who for the sake of *the joy that was set before him* endured the cross, disregarding its shame, and has taken his seat at the right hand of the throne of God. Consider him who endured such hostility against himself from sinners, so that you may not grow weary or lose heart. (Heb 12:1–3)

People regarded Jesus as a loser—an underachiever, a blasphemer, a criminal, a lost cause. Yet, as we read above, Jesus "disregarded" such judgments. Jesus had "joy" amidst disregard. While Jesus was regarded as a loser, he was a joyful loser. Jesus knew that everything in the world was backwards: the purpose of life, how to please God, political aspirations, true happiness—the world had it all 100 percent wrong. Because Jesus did not buy into the way the world thought, but longed only for God and his kingdom, the world hated Jesus and thought of him as a loser. But Jesus had a joy that is beyond circumstances, a joy that enabled him to endure the cruel vengeance of self-centred humanity.

If it is true that Jesus was regarded as a loser, then the Christian must also have no problem (in theory, at least) with being regarded as a loser—but a happy one. It is tragic, but not surprising, that concern with such humility and servanthood is absent in most churches—many officials of which are presumably more interested in maintaining their power and authority than growing in humility. Like the proverbial blind leading the blind, scores of Christians unreflectively follow their "successful" and "victorious" and "charismatic" leaders—at the expense of joyfully being regarded as losers in Jesus.

6

Becoming Ourselves

While it is contrary to wisdom to desire to become like someone else, this does not hold for the ultimate goal of the Christian life—becoming like Jesus. A great paradox is that as we become more fully our ideal selves we cease to be ourselves, for becoming ourselves involves becoming like someone else—becoming like Jesus, who is both the ideal human and the embodiment of our deepest longings. Here are two passages that teach that we are to become like Jesus.

> And all of us, with unveiled faces, seeing the glory of the Lord as though reflected in a mirror, are being transformed into the same image from one degree of glory to another; for this comes from the Lord, the Spirit (2 Cor 3:18).

> Do not lie to one another, seeing that you have stripped off the old self with its practices and have clothed yourselves with the new self, which is being renewed in knowledge according to the image of its creator (Col 3:9–10).

Becoming perfectly ourselves as we become more like Jesus is not an arduous task that involves giving ourselves over to unnatural religious devotion. It is, rather, all about learning to say Yes to life in the kingdom, dispelling the darkness all around us through quiet faith, and growing in love for God and people. Far from being complex, becoming perfectly ourselves is an utterly simple process. The perfect person is one who becomes like Jesus even as they are content to be themselves—no pretence to be someone else, not competing with others, but happy in their own skin before Jesus.

Growing into a greater degree of salvation includes a longing for perfection. The concern with perfection is famously seen in Jesus' counsel to his disciples: "Be perfect, therefore, as your heavenly Father is perfect" (Matt 5:48). As with the many uncomfortable teachings of Jesus, this saying of Jesus has suffered from many attempts to soften its force. The core of the problem revolves around the word *perfect*. In modern English, the word *perfect* is often used with reference to something that has no defects, something that is entirely sound and invincible, or something that is not subject to change and decay. A less common use of the word *perfect* in modern English concerns the goal, end, or objective of something or someone. We say that the end of a compass is to point north. Insofar as a compass fulfills its end, it is perfect. Nothing about the frailty of the compass is here suggested. Yes, the compass may rust over time and lose its ability; yes, humidity, an electrical storm, or a magnetic field may compromise its consistency; but early in its life, and in pristine conditions, the compass fulfilled the task for which it was produced—and it was therefore perfect. It is in this sense that "perfect" of the given verse is to be understood.[1] A paraphrase of the given verse might then be "be perfectly yourself even as God is perfectly himself." Being perfectly oneself is to become like Jesus—full of love and reliance upon God

---

1. A study of how the Greek word that underlies the English word *perfect* is in order. Perhaps the most common interpretation is that *teleios* refers to moral perfection. Some expositors have contended that Jesus is here commanding us to be as purely holy as is God himself. But contrary to this interpretation, I suggest with others that this term refers to completeness or full maturity. In Greek literature outside of the New Testament, *teleios* can refer to animals that have come to full maturity, or even to an object that is in fine working order. The point in such cases is that which is perfect is that which has attained the goal for its existence.

as Father. The disciples of Jesus are perfect insofar as they fulfill in their lives the ultimate end for which God created them. Being perfect has little to do with what one does, and much to do with becoming what God has called one to be. I am here reminded of a portion from the first chapter of the autobiography of St. Thérèse of Lisieux—the "little flower of Jesus."

> Our Lord has deigned to explain this mystery to me. He showed me the book of nature, and I understood that every flower created by Him is beautiful, that the brilliance of the rose and the whiteness of the lily do not lessen the perfume of the violet or the sweet simplicity of the daisy. I understood that if all the lowly flowers wished to be roses, nature would lose its springtide beauty, and the fields would no longer be enamelled with lovely hues. And so it is in the world of souls, Our Lord's living garden. He has been pleased to create great Saints who may be compared to the lily and the rose, but He has also created lesser ones, who must be content to be daisies or simple violets flowering at His Feet, and whose mission it is to gladden His Divine Eyes when He deigns to look down on them. And the more gladly they do His Will the greater is their perfection.[2]

Being perfect is in many respects the opposite of perfectionism, for whether the perfectionist demands perfection from themselves or from another, they are imposing their individual understanding of an ideal. In so doing they are paving the way for judgmentalism—which allows little or no room for people to be themselves. Being perfect thus involves great faith—a faith that has learned that God will draw people to himself, such that we need not get twisted out of shape over what we think someone else ought to be or do or think.

No doubt, on this side of eternity no one can make the claim that they have known such perfection. But the teaching of Jesus never assumes a this-side-of-eternity way of thinking, for the kingdom that is yet to come in its fullness can only be tasted in the here and now. All existence in the here and now is to be shaped

2. Thérèse of Lisieux, *Story*.

by existence in the then and there. It is for this reason that Jesus teaches us to pray, "Your kingdom come, your will be done, on earth as it is in heaven" (Matt 6:10). The kingdom of God has come in Jesus. It follows that our understanding of goodness must be based on the future kingdom that is already here. The Christian is to live their life in accordance with the values of the kingdom that is coming. Being perfectly oneself includes allowing one's understanding of the future kingdom to shape the way in which one presently lives. John says as much in his first letter.

> What we do know is this: when he is revealed, we will be like him, for we will see him as he is. And all who have this hope in him purify themselves, just as he is pure. (1 John 3:2–3)

Becoming perfectly oneself involves many things. Becoming perfect includes becoming pure, which must not be reduced to sexual purity—for purity is based on the awareness that all that is good is from God. When one has this awareness, all existence takes on a life-giving hue. Even as sin and darkness abound, those who are pure in heart choose only to see the beauty of God, for "to the pure, all things are pure" (Titus 1:15). I here remember a debate that I witnessed among theological students. With the exception of one individual, such students agreed that the first lustful look at a scantily dressed and shapely young lady was not a sin—for, it was reasoned, God has wired men to have sexual urges; it is the second lustful look that is a sin—for, it was reasoned, after the first look self-control should kick in. The lone individual corrected the others with his assertion that the first lustful look is a sin, for the pure in heart will only see God-given beauty. Having a pure heart toward others is based on the awareness that all beauty is from God. As such, the Christian does not seek beauty, but God who is the source of beauty. I here think of prayers from two mediaeval nuns.

> God, of your goodness give me yourself for you are sufficient for me. I cannot properly ask anything less, to be worthy of you. If I were to ask less, I should always be in want. In you alone do I have all. (Julian of Norwich)

> You, O eternal Trinity, are a deep sea into which, the more
> I enter, the more I find, and the more I find, the more I
> seek. O abyss, O eternal Godhead, O sea profound, what
> more could you give me than yourself? (Catherine of
> Siena)

Consistent with such prayers, the Christian does not seek greater
purity, but God—who is the source of all virtue.

Becoming perfectly ourselves also involves crucifixion to self.
In many Christian traditions, the crucifixion of Jesus is limited
to what Jesus did for others. While the Christian celebrates that
Jesus died for sinners, limiting the crucifixion to what Jesus did
for others is frightful—for the crucifixion of Jesus is the model of
self-crucifixion, the very pattern of Christian existence. Jesus said
as much:

> If any want to become my followers, let them deny them-
> selves and take up their cross and follow me. For those
> who want to save their life will lose it, and those who lose
> their life for my sake, and for the sake of the gospel, will
> save it. (Mark 8:34–35)

> Whoever wants to become great among you must be
> your servant, and whoever wants to be first must be
> slave of all. For even the Son of Man did not come to be
> served, but to serve, and to give his life as a ransom for
> many. (Mark 10:43–45)

The rest of the New Testament assumes this teaching.

> I have been crucified with Christ; and it is no longer I
> who live, but it is Christ who lives in me (Gal 2:19–20).

> For to this you have been called, because Christ also suf-
> fered for you, leaving you an example, so that you should
> follow in his steps (1 Pet 2:21).

> We know love by this, that he laid down his life for us—
> and we ought to lay down our lives for one another (1
> John 3:16).[3]

3. The resurrection of Christ must also be the Christian's story. Let us here

Profound selfishness has, ironically, been tied to self-crucifixion. I think of much of the monastic movement, in which love of self has dominated—in their mortifications, vows, prayers, and fastings, all too many monks have only loved themselves. Such selfishness can also be seen in individuals who are more concerned with where they will be in eternity than with living for others. (I remember asking a young man if he served Allah because he feared hell. He said yes. I told him that he was then serving himself, not Allah.) This kind of selfishness abounds in those churches that emphasize success and prosperity, in which individuals ask "what is in this for me?" This emphasis is born out of love of self, even as it is furthered by the American dream mentality in which the desires of the individual appear to be more important than anything else. Even salvation becomes a question of "what's in it for me?"

Contrary to "what's in it for me?" thinking, perfection involves dying to self that one may live for God. Dying to oneself is not the same as losing one's essential character—quite the contrary. Years ago I befriended a man who flirted with Buddhism. This man spent many hours in meditation so that he would not become a slave to his desires. While I applauded his efforts, I abhorred the results of his flirtation—for while he did seem to curb his desires, he managed to become subhuman at the same time. What I mean by subhuman is that this man lost his ability to be himself; he lost his individuality, and his death to self was such that he extinguished both desire and identity. Even so, when the Christian dies to self, it is self-centered desire that dies—not one's

---

reflect on the apostle's words: "Do you not know that all of us who have been baptized into Christ Jesus were baptized into his death? Therefore we have been buried with him by baptism into death, so that, just as Christ was raised from the dead by the glory of the Father, so we too might walk in newness of life. For if we have been united with him in a death like his, we will certainly be united with him in a resurrection like his" (Rom 6:3–5); "Now if we are children, then we are heirs—heirs of God and co-heirs with Christ, if indeed we share in his sufferings in order that we may also share in his glory" (Rom 8:17); "We always carry around in our body the death of Jesus, so that the life of Jesus may also be revealed in our body" (2 Cor 4:10). The story of Jesus must become the Christian's story: his crucifixion, and our daily death to self; his resurrection, and our new life.

individuality. One's individuality is never the problem. Love of individuality at the expense of other people is the problem—self-love needs to be converted to love of God at every moment. Insofar as one dies to all the stupidities of vainglory, one will find oneself. I am here reminded of Simone Weil who, at the close of her auto-biography, famously wrote "every time I think of the crucifixion of Christ, I commit the sin of envy." While such a longing to be crucified with Christ is laudatory, many interpreters of Weil's au-tobiography have concluded that, not unlike my Buddhist friend, Weil's desire to be crucified was neurotic—for Weil's desire for self-crucifixion seems to have been wed to her hatred of self. But the Christian is not called to hate oneself, only to die to love of self. The beautiful irony is that as one dies to self, one experiences new life. T. S. Eliot's poem, *The Journey of the Magi*, does a masterful job in capturing this truth: after one of the magi described his difficult journey to the Christ child, and then pondered over the crucifix-ion, the magus asked himself if he was "led all that way for Birth or Death." The magus asserted that the birth of the Christ child brought death to himself: "this Birth was hard and bitter agony for us, like Death, our death." The magus concluded that he "should be glad of another death"—physical death, through which new life can be known.

Perhaps the greatest way in which being perfectly oneself expresses itself is in the area of forgiveness. Forgiveness is not an elective for those who strive to imitate Jesus; forgiveness is integral to what it means to be a Christian. During the Algerian civil war of the 1990s, rebels killed seven Trappist monks. In this story, which also became the motion picture *Of Gods and Men*, the monks demonstrated a profound understanding of Christian discipleship. The monks chose to stay in Algeria even though they were aware that Christians in the country were being killed. Their motivation for staying included being simple instruments of peace in a world ridden with strife. Particularly striking is the monks' forgiveness of those who wronged them. Such forgiveness was stated by the superior of the monastery, Dom Christian, to his would-be killer in his "testament":

In God's face I see yours. May we meet again as happy thieves in Paradise, if it please God, the Father of us both.

There is a wonderful understanding of forgiveness in Dom Christian's words—such that I will use them to discuss what I refer to as the four preconditions of forgiveness.

The first precondition is the recognition that the one whom we are to forgive is entirely human. While this may seem to be so self-evident that it hardly merits discussion, a common feature among those who cannot forgive is the dehumanization of their enemies. Such dehumanization is often seen between warring nations and peoples. During the Second World War, the Japanese were thought by many in the Western world to be animals—"monkeys" in the speech of some. Such thinking is equally present at the individual level, for when we describe our enemies with various slurs or innuendoes we are doing the same as what nations and peoples have done to each other. The psychology behind this practice is simple: if our enemies are less than human, it is more easy to justify our disregard for them.

Coming out of the emphasis that those whom we need to forgive are human is the second precondition of forgiveness: we are equal with our wrongdoers. Earlier in his testament, and with reference both to the wrongdoers as well as those who were wronged, Dom Christian could say "my life is not worth more than any other." Through much of Mahatma Gandhi's autobiography, *The Story of My Experiments with Truth*, Gandhi similarly emphasized that because "all people are painted with the same brush," it would have been wrong for him to think evil of those who were violent toward him—for he would have done precisely the same thing if, like his wrongdoer, he had been led to think in a certain way. If we are to forgive our wrongdoers, we must strive to see that we are equal with them: "Except it be for the grace of God, there go I." Viewing ourselves as being equal with our wrongdoers requires a continuous dose of humility. Such humility involves recognizing our own need for mercy. We must know that, like our wrongdoer, we are mortal and finite. Like everyone else, we are carbon-based life-forms whose very existence depends on the availability of oxygen, water, food, and excretion—and any ability that we have has everything to do with the goodness of God in our lives.

I here think of my own struggle to forgive. I have had a very hard time forgiving a pastor who decades ago was sexually unbecoming toward me. I will spare the reader the sordid details. What I have learned from this negative experience is that forgiveness must be ongoing—for even though I have forgiven the pastor, from time to time the anger wells up in me. Some years ago a friend asked me if I forgave this pastor. I responded with "there is nothing to forgive; I am him." The point that I was making is that even while I think that what the pastor said and did was sick to the core, I cannot judge him as if I am better than him—for if I care to look deep enough into my own heart I will also find seeds of destructiveness, seeds that the pastor allowed to germinate in his heart. But were I to be asked the same question at another time (i.e., if I forgave the pastor), my answer might not be as generous. Like any virtue, there is an iterative quality to forgiveness: we must forgive over and over—and as we progress in forgiveness, it becomes easier to forgive.

The third precondition of forgiveness is that we need to recognize the image of God within our wrongdoers. This is implicit in Dom Christian's words, "In God's face I see yours." Just as the basis for true compassion is seeing the God-given worth of every individual, so the basis of forgiveness is growing in the ability to see the image of God even in those who wrong us. In *The Hiding Place*, Corrie ten Boom writes of how, while a female Nazi guard brutally beat an inmate, her sister Betsie said, "I feel sorry for her." Corrie mistakenly thought that Betsie was referring to the beaten inmate, but Betsie actually felt sorry for the guard who did the beating. Like Betsie, Oscar Romero, who strove to follow Jesus even in the midst of persecution in El Salvador, emphasized that all people—victims and victimizers alike—bear the image of God. While the meaning of the phrase "image of God" has been widely debated, it is generally agreed that this phrase refers to the divine worth of every individual. Pure love for any individual involves loving, paradoxically, not them, but the image of God within them. Loving other people is therefore a thoroughgoing religious act. Loving others is one with loving God, for every individual is a representative of God—irrespective of the way that the image of God within them might be besmirched. Conversely, violating any person in some way is to violate God himself. Jesus' teaching about this matter is explicit in the parable of the sheep and goats in Matthew 25—"whatever you did to one of the least of these, you did to me." With reference to the subject of forgiveness, God forgives us as we forgive others: "forgive us our trespasses as we forgive those who trespass against us" (Matt 6:12). If we are rich in mercy, the mercy of God will likewise wash over us: "blessed are the merciful, for they shall receive mercy" (Matt 5:7). In this sense, we are creating our own eternity in the way that we treat others—and the realization that every individual bears the image of God ought to motivate us to grow in virtue.

The fourth precondition for forgiveness involves immersing oneself in the forgiveness of God. The Christian's ability to forgive others is proportionate to their understanding of how God has forgiven them. This is implied in the following counsel.

> Forgive each other. Just as the Lord has forgiven you, so you also must forgive. (Col 3:13)

That one's forgiveness of others is to parallel how God has forgiven them is the point of the parable of the unmerciful servant in Matthew 18.

> For this reason the kingdom of heaven may be compared to a king who wished to settle accounts with his slaves. When he began the reckoning, one who owed him ten thousand talents was brought to him; and, as he could not pay, his lord ordered him to be sold, together with his wife and children and all his possessions, and payment to be made. So the slave fell on his knees before him, saying, "Have patience with me, and I will pay you everything." And out of pity for him, the lord of that slave released him and forgave him the debt. But that same slave, as he went out, came upon one of his fellow slaves who owed him a hundred denarii; and seizing him by the throat, he

said, "Pay what you owe." Then his fellow slave fell down
and pleaded with him, "Have patience with me, and I
will pay you." But he refused; then he went and threw
him into prison until he would pay the debt. When his
fellow slaves saw what had happened, they were greatly
distressed, and they went and reported to their lord all
that had taken place. Then his lord summoned him and
said to him, "You wicked slave! I forgave you all that debt
because you pleaded with me. Should you not have had
mercy on your fellow slave, as I had mercy on you?" And
in anger his lord handed him over to be tortured until
he would pay his entire debt. So my heavenly Father will
also do to every one of you, if you do not forgive your
brother or sister from your heart.

The power of this parable hinges on the ridiculous sum of
money that the first slave owed his lord compared to the paltry
sum that the second slave owed the first slave. One learns from
Josephus (a first-century Jewish historian) that Judea's annual tax
to Rome in the early first century amounted to about 500 talents.
The 10,000 talents that the first slave owed his lord amounted to
20 times as much as this—more than 150,000 years of wages for
a laborer. Upon being told to repay this gargantuan sum, the first
slave desperately declared that he would repay everything that he
owed the king—which was not remotely possible. In his mercy,
the king forgave the entire debt of this slave. But when this same
slave saw a fellow slave who owed him 100 denarii (one denarius
was a day's wages), unlike the way that his lord had treated him, he
refused to have mercy on his fellow slave. When the merciful lord
heard of this, he became enraged and sent the unforgiving slave
to prison. Jesus concluded the parable with this drastic teaching:
"So my heavenly Father will also do to every one of you, if you do
not forgive your brother or sister from your heart." I say "drastic"
intentionally, for there is nothing more difficult than learning not
simply to forgive others, but to do so from one's heart.

This brings us to the topic of self-forgiveness. I have often
heard well-meaning people say, "I can forgive others, but I cannot
forgive myself." As in so many matters, the issue is not the issue, for

the topic itself is not based on faith but on modern psychological theory, which suggests that the self cannot practice virtue when it is dysfunctional. The fundamental problem with such theory concerns the understanding of self. Unlike modern psychological theory, the follower of Jesus is concerned with how the self is to die. One must carefully reflect, then, on the statement "I can forgive others, but I cannot forgive myself." While the intentions may be sound, striving to forgive oneself has little to do with Christian faith and much to do with self-centered thinking. Like any virtue, forgiveness is not grounded in self but in God: we love because God is love; we are humble because God is humble—and we forgive because God forgives. The follower of Jesus does not seek the ability to forgive, but God who forgives. Indeed, the Bible never exhorts us to forgive ourselves, for the subject of self-forgiveness is simply not part of the equation. The statement, "I cannot forgive myself" is simply not consistent with Christian thinking. It is only the marriage of modern psychology and popular theology that has brought the subject of self-forgiveness to the fore.

These, then, are the four preconditions to forgiveness: the recognition that the one whom we must forgive is entirely human; being aware that we are equal with our wrongdoers; knowing that the image of God is borne by our wrongdoers; and imitating the way in which God has forgiven us. The degree to which we fulfill such preconditions in our hearts will determine the degree to which we truly forgive. Insofar as we do not long to have such preconditions met in our hearts, our forgiveness of others may only amount to words. We may say "I forgive you," but if our hearts have not been changed such words might only be empty platitudes. I here think of the acronym WWJD, which stands for "what would Jesus do?" Consonant with many fads in society, for a number of years this acronym was seen on bracelets, bumper stickers, T-shirts, and it was even tattooed on bodies. I celebrate this fad. All the same, a careful reading of the Gospels tells us that the acronym might well have been WWJB—that is, "who would Jesus be?" Being a disciple is not first and foremost about changing one's behavior, but having one's heart transformed. So also, forgiveness is not about mouthing

words such as "I forgive you," but having our hearts transformed—
such that we love those who have hurt us.

One way in which forgiveness ought to manifest itself in
our lives is that we should want the very best for those who have
wronged us. Contrary to the thinking of many, true forgiveness is
not simply making things right between ourselves and our wrongdoers. Complete forgiveness goes much further insofar as it wants
the very best for wrongdoers. Some time ago, I spent time with
a young man who carried around a hit list with him. On this list
were people who had wronged him in the past whom he wanted
to murder prior to killing himself. People on the list included
high-school bullies, so-called friends who seduced his wife, and
those who cheated him out of money. After gaining a measure of
rapport with this young man, I encouraged him to take his hit list
and begin to pray a blessing on each person on the list. I told him
that as he did so his heart would change toward his enemies. I also
told him that he would help himself as he forgave those who had
wronged him—for so long as the anger that we have toward others
is nurtured, we are killing our own souls. We must want the very
best for those who have wronged us, such that we should strive
not to have any enemies. People may well regard us as enemies,
and perhaps this cannot be avoided, but the Christian must not
regard anyone as an enemy. I feel sorry for those psalmists who
were wildly distraught because of their enemies. Here are a few
examples.

> How long must I bear pain in my soul, and have sorrow
> in my heart all day long? How long shall my enemy be
> exalted over me? (Ps 13:2)

> Why must I walk about mournfully because the enemy
> oppresses me? (Ps 42:9).

> I am distraught by the noise of the enemy, because of the
> clamour of the wicked. For they bring trouble upon me,
> and in anger they cherish enmity against me. My heart
> is in anguish within me, the terrors of death have fallen

upon me. Fear and trembling come upon me, and horror overwhelms me. (Ps 55:2–5).

Such sentiments are typical in the psalms, even as other psalms suggest that entertaining such enmity is not conducive to purity of heart. The conclusion of Psalm 139 is instructive in this regard, for after this psalmist says "I hate them with perfect hatred; I count them my enemies," almost as if to confess such an attitude, the psalmist piously prays, "Search me, O God, and know my heart; test me and know my thoughts. See if there is any wicked way in me, and lead me in the way everlasting."

With the teaching of Jesus we move from hatred of one's enemies to boundless mercy toward them. Just prior to the parable of the Unmerciful Servant (which we looked at above), there is the following dialogue between Peter and Jesus.

> Then Peter came and said to him, "Lord, if another member of the church sins against me, how often should I forgive? As many as seven times?" Jesus said to him, "Not seven times, but, I tell you, *seventy-seven times.*" (Matt 18:21–22)

Jesus' use of "seventy-seven times" is an allusion to the murderous words of Lamech.

> Adah and Zillah, hear my voice; you wives of Lamech, listen to what I say: I have killed a man for wounding me, a young man for striking me. If Cain is avenged seven times over, truly Lamech *seventy-seven times* over. (Gen 4:23–24).

By means of this allusion, Jesus taught that just as Lamech expressed perfect vengeance to a man who slighted him, so followers of Jesus are to express perfect mercy toward those who wrong them. These were not just words for Jesus, for he himself embodied his emphasis on desiring mercy for all people. This is particularly seen in his cry to God for the forgiveness of those who mocked and crucified him: "Father, forgive them, for they do not know what they are doing" (Luke 23:34).

A modern caveat to boundless forgiveness is expressed in the following way: "God has not called us to be doormats. Yes, we are to forgive, but we must not put up with unjustified abuse, for doing so is to enable those who wrong us." I concur. God has not called us to be doormats . . . but happy doormats! With Jesus, Christians are happily to pray for and bless those who have wronged them—through maligning, insult, contempt, abuse, manipulation, and scores of other injustices. To seek refuge behind the "enabling" argument is to cease to follow the way of Jesus. Being a happy doormat is not to be equated with enabling the wrongdoer: indeed, let the wrongdoer be called to account, but let our primary concern always be the condition of our hearts toward a wrongdoer—never on the injustice that has come our way. Paul similarly exhorted the Corinthians who were taking each other to court over injustices: "why not rather be wronged?" (1 Cor 6:7). Disciples of Jesus learn that the way of forgiveness, not justice, is the way of life—even as James could teach: "mercy triumphs over judgment" (Jas 2:13).

A fine example of imitating Jesus in forgiveness concerns the martyrdom of Stephen, one of the first members of the Way to be executed.

> While they were stoning Stephen, he prayed, "Lord Jesus, receive my spirit." Then he knelt down and cried out in a loud voice, "Lord, do not hold this sin against them." When he had said this, he died. (Act 7:59–60)

Correspondences between the death of Jesus and the martyrdom of Stephen are striking: as Jesus petitioned his Father with "into your hands I commend my spirit" (Luke 23:46), so Stephen asked Jesus to receive his spirit; and as Jesus prayed "Father, forgive them; for they do not know what they are doing" (Luke 23:34), so Stephen asked Jesus to forgive those who were stoning him. As with Stephen's death, church history tells us stories of many individuals who understood their sufferings through the sufferings of Jesus.

Conclusion:
Reflections on 1 Corinthians 13

The love chapter, 1 Corinthians 13, brings together much of what I have been trying to say in this book. Prior to looking at the love chapter, we would do well to note again that the New Testament teaches that love is supreme—and we worship God only insofar as we love. When an "expert in the law" asked Jesus what the greatest commandment was, Jesus gave two quotations from the Books of Moses:

> "Love the Lord your God with all your heart and with all your soul and with all your mind." This is the first and greatest commandment. And the second is like it: "Love your neighbour as yourself." All the Law and the Prophets hang on these two commandments. (Matt 22:37–40)

Paul similarly counseled the Romans: "Love does no harm to a neighbour; love is therefore the fulfillment of the law" (Rom 13:10), even as he told the Galatians that "the entire law is fulfilled in keeping this one command: 'Love your neighbour as yourself'" (Gal 5:14). The author of 1 Peter likewise told his readers that above all else they were to "maintain constant love for one another, for love covers a multitude of sins" (1 Pet 4:8).

Knowing the historical and literary contexts of the love chapter will assist the reader in understanding it. The historical context is that Paul had started a church in the port city of Corinth. As with most churches that Paul founded, this church met in a home.

The home belonged to a woman named Chloe. Some time after Paul left Corinth, members from this church visited Paul. This delegation carried a letter in which members of the Corinthian church asked Paul various questions. Paul wrote much of 1 Corinthians in response to such questions. One question concerned "spiritual gifts"—speaking in tongues, prophesying, and the like. The careless practice of such spiritual gifts led to divisions within the church. Paul addressed this matter in chapters 12 and 14. The literary context of the love chapter is also important to see. Chapter 13 is parenthetical to chapters 12 and 14. As Paul did in other letters, in this parenthesis he interrupted himself to emphasize something that is vitally important. In this case, what Paul thought was essential is that the Corinthian believers understood spiritual gifts in light of love—spiritual gifts have no value whatsoever if such gifts do not further the love of God in Jesus. The parenthetical nature of the love discourse is also seen in the way that it is sandwiched by what is the most "excellent" and "greatest": at the beginning of his discourse Paul said, "I will show you a still more excellent way", and at the end of his discourse he said, "the greatest of these is love."

Here is the love chapter.[1]

> 31b Now I will show you the most excellent way. 1 If I speak in the tongues of mortals and of angels, but do not have love, I am a noisy gong or a clanging cymbal. 2 And if I have prophetic powers, and understand all mysteries and all knowledge, and if I have all faith, so as to remove mountains, but do not have love, I am nothing. 3 If I give away all my possessions, and if I hand over my body so that I may boast, but do not have love, I gain nothing. 4 Love is patient; love is kind; love is not envious or boastful or arrogant 5 or rude. It does not insist on its own way; it is not irritable or resentful; 6 it does not rejoice in wrongdoing, but rejoices in the truth. 7 It bears all

---

1. I have included the last half-verse of chapter 12 in the love chapter, for this half-verse introduces the subject of love. (A joke has been made that the one who introduced the chapter and verse divisions did so on an ox cart on a bumpy road—such that the divisions are sometimes careless.)

things, believes all things, hopes all things, endures all things. 8 Love never ends. But as for prophecies, they will come to an end; as for tongues, they will cease; as for knowledge, it will come to an end. 9 For we know only in part, and we prophesy only in part; 10 but when the complete comes, the partial will come to an end. 11 When I was a child, I spoke like a child, I thought like a child, I reasoned like a child; when I became an adult, I put an end to childish ways. 12 For now we see in a mirror, dimly, but then we will see face to face. Now I know only in part; then I will know fully, even as I have been fully known. 13 And now faith, hope, and love abide, these three; and the greatest of these is love.

The love chapter consists of three sections, the first of which (verses 1–3) concerns the supremacy of love. God gave the Corinthians spiritual gifts that enabled them to prosper in their faith. Presumably in states of religious ecstasy, many of the Corinthians spoke in different tongues as they prayed and worshipped. Paul thanked God that the Corinthians had this gift—even as he told them he wished that all people could have this experience, and that he spoke in tongues more than any of the Corinthians. But as wonderful as speaking in tongues might have been, Paul taught that the practice of this gift only had merit if it was guided by love for others. It is for this reason that Paul told the Corinthians that he would rather speak 10,000 intelligible words than five words in a tongue that no one else could understand. Insofar as speaking in tongues was not propelled by love, the practice of this gift in a formal worship setting only amounted to cacophony—an irritating sound akin to "a noisy gong or a clanging cymbal." What Paul taught about speaking in tongues was equally true of other spiritual gifts. Whether it be prophetic powers, words of knowledge, or faith that could produce miracles—all Spirit-given abilities had merit only insofar as they were governed by love. Verse three moves the discussion to the supremacy of love over sacrifices: like the supremacy of love over spiritual gifts, both sacrificial giving (even giving everything that one owns), and sacrificing oneself as a martyr (even dying in the flames) only have significance when they are led by love.

In the second section (verses 4–7), the apostle provides a list that describes love. This list is not meant to be definitive, for love defies definition. Because God himself is beyond what words can describe, any attempt to define God's love will similarly fall short. Even the crucifixion of Jesus—which is the supreme example of love—is not a definition. John tells us that we know what love looks like: "Jesus Christ laid down his life for us" (1 John 3:16). But John is here telling us the fruit of love, not the nature of love: love itself, and not how love manifests itself, is beyond what any book might say about it. Even when the Bible comes close to defining love, as in the love chapter, it quickly acknowledges that love is inexpressible: the love chapter states that in the here and now we only "know in part," and that "we only see a reflection" of truth—not the full truth itself. All the same, we can have a foretaste of eternal truth if we abide in love—a truth that must be experienced to be known. We might know something about God through careful definitions, but we can only know God himself as we live in the love of God.

The third section (verses 8–12) concerns the eternal nature of love. Whereas the practice of the spiritual gifts will come to an end, love will never cease. Paul here suggests that all things find their fulfillment in love—for while the spiritual gifts point to love, such a love will only be fully realized in eternity.

Inasmuch as mortal love is an image of immortal Love, these verses suggest that love is rather Platonic. What is true of love equally holds for all virtue: virtue in this world is only genuine when it is grounded in the Virtue that is above—only God is good, and all goodness is therefore but a reflection of God. This is precisely the case with love, for the only love that exists is the love of God—and all expressions of love find their fulfillment in Love. I said above that love is "rather" Platonic. The difference between love and the forms of Platonism is that the latter allow little room for change—Platonic forms are essentially static. Contrary to the forms of Platonic thought, love is ever-changing. Insofar as love seeks to meet different needs of different people at different times, love participates in the changing nature of reality. The adaptation of love in different situations is assumed everywhere in the New Testament: it is assumed in the incarnation of God in Jesus; and it is present in the ministry of Paul—who became a Jew to the Jews, a Greek to the Greeks, and who was weak to those who are weak (1 Cor 9:20–22). The changing nature of love is also exemplified in the apostle's counsel to the Corinthians regarding food sacrificed to idols in 1 Corinthians 8 and 10. Those believers with "knowledge" must not get "puffed up" with pride, but must build up others through love. The knowledge that one has that it is not sinful to eat meat that had been sacrificed to idols must be wary that such knowledge does not cause the weak to stumble in their faith. Far from being static, love must consider what is good and right in every situation.

Complementing its changing nature, love is also evolutionary. The evolutionary nature of love is suggested by the use of the metaphor of growing into adulthood: "When I was a child, I spoke like a child, I thought like a child, I reasoned like a child; when I became an adult, I put an end to childish ways" (verse 11). This metaphor is similarly used elsewhere in the New Testament.

> Brothers and sisters, I could not address you as people who live by the Spirit but as people who are still worldly—mere infants in Christ. I gave you milk, not solid food, for you were not yet ready for it. Indeed, you are still not ready. (1 Cor 3:1–2)

> You need someone to teach you the elementary truths of God's word all over again. You need milk, not solid food! Anyone who lives on milk, being still an infant, is not acquainted with the teaching about righteousness. But solid food is for the mature. (Heb 5:12–14)

The fundamental problem is rarely that one has the wrong view on something, or that one's lifestyle is counter to faith—for such problems can be addressed and changed. A root problem exists when one stops progressing in salvation. The author of 1 Peter wrote the following: "Like newborn babies, crave pure spiritual milk, so that by it you may grow up in your salvation" (1 Pet 2:2). Contrary to such progress, salvation might be slowed or even halted when the disciple approaches faith as though it were static and unchanging. Their thinking might be that their church or their doctrine is all that they need; and because their church is the true one, or because their doctrine cannot be improved upon, their faith becomes stagnant. Like the evolutionary nature of salvation, love must also evolve. The evolutionary nature of love is tied to the constant transformation that all followers of Jesus experience, for growth in the kingdom is a process in which the Spirit of God enables the disciple to become a new creation: usually slowly, sometimes quickly, but always moving toward one's true self—which is found in Christ.

Along the journey, the disciple might note that their understanding of love has evolved. I am here reminded of how my view regarding the drinking of alcohol has changed. When I first became a Christian, I thought that any form of drinking alcohol was a sin. I remember seeing Christians enjoying wine at a meal in a restaurant, and I judged them accordingly. I eventually became more broad-minded, such that I could tolerate drinking in others, but I would not drink myself. Years later I myself enjoyed the occasional beer or wine. When I became the president of a seminary in Nigeria, I warned my students that if I caught any of them drinking beer I would immediately expel them (I would not have done so, but I needed to sound tough). In the same breath, I told the Nigerian students that when I returned to Canada, I would go to the pub with my friends and enjoy a beer. I taught my students that there is nothing at all hypocritical about this, for context is everything: in that region of Nigeria, one only drank the terrible-tasting brew to get drunk; but among my friends in Canada, drinking a tasty beer in a pub with friends was good fun. The evolution of love came to a fuller expression in more recent years when I started a ministry in a pub, which was affectionately referred to as "Jesus on Tap." Every month Christians and others (many of whom were disenchanted with organized religion) would get together at the pub to discuss one or another teaching of

Jesus. I have since concluded that not having a beer can be as much an offence as having a beer. I have seen unbelievers getting turned off simply because they have equated Christian faith with kill-joy Christianity. As well-meaning as they might be, legalistic and immature Christians must know that "the kingdom of God is not a matter of eating and drinking, but of righteousness, peace and joy in the Holy Spirit" (Rom 14:17). At the beginning of my journey, then, as I learned to crawl, I needed a list of do's and dont's—a list that was conveniently located in a book.[2] As I continued in the journey and wanted to walk and then run, this list became insufficient—such that I began to put more confidence in God who has been bringing me to himself.

Given that love is ever-changing and that it is evolutionary, we must not take ourselves too seriously. All that we take in a deadly serious manner is whether or not we are living in love. I need to remind myself not to take myself too seriously. Not long ago I received a life-sized x-ray of my chest from the hospital, which I taped to my window. Every day I look at the x-ray to remind myself that I am mostly made of water, and it is silly to take myself too seriously. As with all things that dissolve and decay, the x-ray has since faded, and it is no longer on my window. But because my tendency to take myself too seriously still crops up, I now have another method to remind myself not to take myself too seriously. The apostle teaches that while he is serious about the kingdom, he holds onto all things lightly. Let us, with the apostle, have a light touch that is also firm: light insofar as we do not get bent out of shape over tiny matters, but firm insofar as we are serious about the transformation of our hearts.

---

2. People want a book that will answer their questions about love—what is the nature of love, how to love, what deeds are loving, etc. But love cannot be codified. Were a comprehensive book about love to exist, it would be trillions of pages long, for love has a chameleon-like nature insofar as it changes for every individual in every situation. Such a book would also be in constant need of revision and updating—for what is loving in one time or circumstance is not necessarily loving in another time or circumstance. No such book exists or even could exist.

In addition to being a noun, love is a verb. It requires action. Love itself shapes knowing and doing, even as knowing and doing together shape love. The members of the knowing-doing-being triad thus work in harmony, even as they find their fulfillment in love. The fact that love is a verb has very real consequences for an understanding of daily life. When we walk in love, our knowledge of love increases—as does our ability to do loving things. Whether it is being stuck in traffic, overhearing gossip in the office, eating a less-than-appetizing lunch, or cleaning off the dinner table, the concern of love is ever before the follower of Jesus. Nothing in life (however mundane and this-worldly it might seem to be) escapes love. Indeed, the more that one grows in love, the less that one makes a distinction between the mundane and the supra-mundane, between the sacred and the profane, between this world and the next—for when one lives in love, all of existence becomes holy. The apostle's teaching that all things are "from" and "through" and "for" God are not empty abstractions to the one who lives in love.

> For from him and through him and for him are all things (Rom 11:36).

> There is but one God, the Father, from whom all things came and for whom we live; and there is but one Lord, Jesus Christ, through whom all things came and through whom we live (1 Cor 8:6).

When one lives in the love of God, the prepositions "from," "through," and "for" suggest that the believer is an instrument of God in every setting. Everything that we do is sacred—for we see God everywhere; and neither the daily grind of existence, nor the feverish pace of life are exceptions.

People often say that they do not have time for God, or, perhaps better, they say that they must make time for God. Such people have a childish faith—for those who have eyes to see can see the kingdom everywhere and in all things. Not having time for God is to assume a distinction between the sacred and the secular. For the believer, everything is sacred. One cannot make time for God, for God is always and continuously present. Even as Brother Lawrence of the Resurrection taught, God is equally present everywhere—in the peeling of potatoes and in prayer, in mending shoes and in the mass. People of mature faith find God equally in the sanctuary and in the shopping mall, in the chapel and at a hockey practice, in the pages of the Bible and in a pub, in prayer and in helping a child with homework. Subjects of the kingdom see the kingdom everywhere—in all people, and in all situations. As such, the traditional divide between the sacred and the secular collapses. To the one who has eyes that can see, everything is sacred—for the kingdom of God penetrates all time and space. The subsuming of the secular into the sacred is implicit in God becoming human. The collapse of the secular into the sacred is similarly seen in the rending of the curtain of the temple: no longer is there a divide between the Holy of Holies and secular existence, for through the Christ event the sacred nature of all existence has become manifest. A very real challenge therefore exists for any religious tradition that makes a distinction between formal worship and daily life. One cannot leave secular space to enter into sacred space, for all space is equally sacred. God is no more present at the consecration of the host than he is when sandwiches are given to the poor at a mission, or when a baby's diaper is changed.[3]

Verse 13 concludes the love chapter, even as it suggests that a relationship exists between faith, hope, and love. In three instances Paul included the three together.

> And now *faith*, *hope*, and *love* abide, these three; and the greatest of these is love (1 Cor 13:13).

> We always give thanks to God for all of you and mention you in our prayers, constantly remembering before our God and Father your work of *faith* and labour of *love* and steadfastness of *hope* in our Lord Jesus Christ (1 Thess 1:2–3).

---

3. I am not at all undermining the need for formal worship. I am only suggesting that the merit of such worship is tied to the way that it compels the believer to worship at all times, in all places, and in all actions.

> But since we belong to the day, let us be sober, and put on
> the breastplate of *faith* and *love*, and for a helmet the *hope*
> of salvation (1 Thess 5:8).

The relationship between faith, hope, and love is exquisite. Faith gives rise to hope, even as both faith and hope find their basis in the love of God. This movement between faith, hope, and love spans this world even as it allows us to have a foretaste of the world to come—for just as all three are together rooted in this world, they all participate in the love that infuses both this world and the next. I will now say more about how faith, hope, and love are interrelated.

I first note that the word *faith* has a nuance of "trust." Saying that one has faith in God is at the same time saying that one trusts in God. Churches have often communicated that faith is propositional. According to this perspective, faith concerns mental ascent: one believes insofar as one mentally concurs with a set of religious propositions—such as a creed, a statement of faith, or a catechism. While creeds, statements of faith, and catechisms do have legitimate functions, confusing mental agreement with faith is most unfortunate, for doing so leaves little room for trust. That faith has a nuance of trust is also clear from how the verb "believe" (*pisteuō*) is used in the New Testament. Certainly one of the most-loved verses in the Bible is John 3:16.

> For God so loved the world that he gave his only Son,
> so that everyone who *believes* in him may not perish but
> may have eternal life.

While I happily concur that this verse summarizes much of the gospel, the nuance of "trust" that resides in "believe" in this verse is usually overlooked. That "believe" here has a nuance of "trust" is evident from the use of this word a little earlier—"Jesus on his part would not *entrust* himself to them, because he knew all people" (John 2:24). Far from simply assenting to a religious decree, faith involves trusting. This observation has a huge impact on how one receives the gospel, for such reception is then not just creedal, but life-changing. The believer does not trust in anything that the world affords, not political stability, not health of body and mind, not a familial relationship, not a decent bank account, not their health, not even in any gift from God. The believer does not ultimately trust in any thing, but only in God. Even when everything seems to be falling apart, the believer rests in the assurance that nothing can take them from the love of God.

Faith also knows that it must be shaped by love; and love looks different for every individual and in every differing circumstance. It is for this reason that the New Testament often disregards teachings that are not grounded in love. I here draw our attention to the apostle's teaching to the church in Rome. In Romans 14, Paul tells the Romans not to quarrel over disputable matters—such as eating meat, drinking wine, or observing sacred days. More important to God than having the correct opinion is accepting one another. As I noted above, Paul similarly exhorted the Corinthians to abstain from eating meat that had been sacrificed to idols. While Paul implied that people who did not eat meat (because doing so was thought to compromise the faith) were immature, he nevertheless counseled those who were more mature not to eat such meat— lest they be "stumbling blocks" to those who are immature. In all situations, a faith that is shaped by love trumps every other consideration. What Paul told the Romans and the Corinthians may equally be applied to what he told the Galatians—many Galatian Christians regarded circumcision as the litmus test of true faith. Paul counseled the Galatians that "the only thing that counts is faith expressing itself through love" (Gal 5:6).[4] The apostle taught that sin is not an act that is contrary to a decree, but an act that does not proceed from a faith that is shaped by love. Sin is not, first and foremost, what one does or does not do—for doing or not doing something is the fruit of sin, not sin itself. It is for this reason that the apostle spoke of the sinful desires of the flesh—actions are the consequence of sinful desire. This teaching is also implicit in Jesus' challenge to Mosaic thinking in the Sermon on the Mount: it

---

4. I am here reminded of a saying that has been attributed to Augustine: "In disputable matters, liberty; in indisputable matters, unity; and in all things, charity."

is not breaking a commandment that is the problem, but the condition of the heart that leads to the breaking of the commandment.

Kierkegaard made a similar point in *Fear and Trembling*. In his discussion of the ethical nature of Abraham's sacrifice of Isaac, Kierkegaard contended that, in terms of ethics, Abraham must be regarded as a murderer, but in terms of religious commitment, Abraham must be regarded as a man of faith. According to Kierkegaard, this paradox contains the very stuff of faith. Faith is not first and foremost concurrence with an outer, objective, imperative (e.g., a command in the Bible), but concurrence with the inner, subjective voice of God-given conscience. Stated otherwise, while in terms of objective ethic Abraham may have been a murderer, in terms of the subjective voice of conscience Abraham was a man of faith. We learn from Abraham that the concern of faith is not about being consistent with a code of conduct, but following the voice of a transformed conscience. There is no doubt that this provides a slippery slope, for if the life of faith ultimately involves favoring the voice of conscience over any objective imperative, it might seem that the way has been paved for justifying oneself for doing something that is wrong. Happily, however, faith has checks and balances that keep it honest. One such balance is love: faith is true only when it is suffused with love, and insofar as faith leads to an action that is not explicable by love for God, such a faith is untrue. Another balance is humility: faith is only true when it is undergirded by humility, and insofar as faith leads to an action that is no grounded in humility, such a faith is similarly untrue. Akin to the conclusions of Kierkegaard are those of Joseph Fletcher in his *Situation Ethics*. Fletcher contended that all commands are to be obeyed relative to circumstances. While in the vast majority of instances the gist of individual commands are to be obeyed, there are some instances in which obeying one command is to disobey the command to love. One thinks, for example, of the prohibition against lying and the story of how the Hebrew midwives lied about the male infants in Exodus 1. The midwives told Pharaoh that they did not kill the male infants because the Hebrew women gave birth before they arrived to assist them with the delivery. Far from chastising the midwives for this deception, God rewarded them for lying—for insofar as they disobeyed the prohibition against lying, they obeyed the command to love. Not unlike Kierkegaard's suspension of the ethical, situation ethics has wrongly been equated with antinomianism ("against law") or libertinism ("freedom from moral constraints"). Such criticisms are most inaccurate, for Fletcher and others have emphasized that the ethical nature of all deeds is proportionate to the love that empowers them.

I now turn to a discussion of hope. I first note that faith and hope are tied together. Where faith concerns what will take place in the future, hope actualizes this future in the present. Just as the existence of a mature oak tree is present in the acorn from which the oak tree emerges, so the existence of hope is present in God's promises of the future. Faith necessarily produces hope, and hope is the realization of faith. Where faith says, "this will happen," hope says, "present existence must be shaped by knowing that this will happen." As such, hope may simply be defined as *how an understanding of the future shapes the present.* Insofar as hope involves how the future shapes the present, there is an eschatological aspect to hope. This eschatological aspect is known as "realized eschatology." According to realized eschatology, the future kingdom exists already in the present kingdom. This perspective is seen in the following examples from the Gospel of John.

> Very truly, I tell you, anyone who hears my word and believes him who sent me has eternal life, and does not come under judgment, but has passed from death to life. Very truly, I tell you, the hour is coming, and is now here, when the dead will hear the voice of the Son of God, and those who hear will live. (John 5:24–25)

> Martha said to Jesus, "Lord, if you had been here, my brother would not have died. But even now I know that God will give you whatever you ask of him." Jesus said to her, "Your brother will rise again." Martha said to him, "I know that he will rise again in the resurrection on the last day." Jesus said to her, "I am the resurrection and the life. Those who believe in me, even though they die,

will live, and everyone who lives and believes in me will
never die. Do you believe this?" (John 11:21–26)

While they will physically die, those who believe in Jesus will
not spiritually die, for they have passed from spiritual death to
spiritual life. Present existence participates in the future, even as it
anticipates it. The ethic of Jesus must similarly be seen in light of
realized eschatology. Jesus suggested as much in his prayer: "your
kingdom come, your will be done, on earth as it is in heaven" (Matt
6:10). Disciples are to practice mercy in this life even as they wish
to receive mercy in the next, they are to refrain from judging in the
here and now lest they be judged in the there and then, and if they
forgive in this world they will be forgiven in the world to come.
Together with much of Jesus' teachings, the Beatitudes of Matthew
5 are to be understood with reference to realized eschatology, for
six of the nine beatitudes begin with a virtue that is presently prac-
ticed even as they conclude with a future reward.

> Blessed are those who mourn, for they *will be* comforted.
>
> Blessed are the meek, for they *will* inherit the earth.
>
> Blessed are those who hunger and thirst for righteousness, for
> they *will be* filled.
>
> Blessed are the merciful, for they *will* receive mercy.
>
> Blessed are the pure in heart, for they *will* see God.
>
> Blessed are the peacemakers, for they *will* be called children
> of God.

A simple reading of such beatitudes might lead one to conclude
that Jesus created a dichotomy between present virtue and future
reward. But such a conclusion would be unwarranted, for two of
the remaining beatitudes underline the fact that present virtue
brings one into "the kingdom of heaven" in the here and now.

> Blessed are the poor in spirit, for theirs is *the kingdom
> of heaven.*
>
> Blessed are those who are persecuted for righteousness'
> sake, for theirs is *the kingdom of heaven.*

Elsewhere in the Gospels, one learns that the kingdom of heaven began already with the proclamation of Jesus. Motivation for virtue is thus tied to entrance into the kingdom of heaven in the here and now—even as it is known that the promise will only be fully realized in the hereafter. The teaching of Jesus is thus consistent with the eschatological nature of hope, for being a child of the future kingdom shapes and defines present existence. I here think of the words of Thérèse of Lisieux: "I want to spend my heaven doing good on earth." For those who are guided by hope, heavenly existence merges with earthly existence, and the life of virtue involves mirroring heaven's virtue in one's present existence.

Consistent with the subject of hope is the subject of theological optimism. Theological optimism is not to be confused with optimism in general. Secular optimism is all about looking for and seeing the best in a difficult situation. Such optimism appears in various slogans such as "when life serves you lemons, make lemonade." But slogans like this are painfully sugar-coated. Shall we counsel the young woman who is forced to fetch water ten kilometres from her home (even as she worries about getting raped on the way) to put a skip in her step and hum "What a Wonderful World"? Secular optimism says that the young woman's fundamental problem is not that she is dying from AIDS, not that her uneducated children have been unfed for two days, and not that her teenage son has become a child soldier. Her one problem is that she is not positive enough. The young woman really ought to read *The Power of Positive Thinking* or one of the self-help books that occupy the shelves of the local bookstore. The young woman would do well to follow the sage counsel of afternoon talk show hosts. This sort of optimism that thrives in the Western world today is hopelessly ethnocentric and self-serving. Theological optimism is also to be distinguished from theological pessimism, which stresses the sinfulness and spiritual darkness of every individual and society. I recoil at this emphasis, for all too often those who subscribe to one form or another of theological pessimism have little understanding of the mercy of God in Jesus Christ. Yes, humanity is enslaved to sin and darkness at every level—be it individual depravity or the structural evils that abound in society. But this is only one chapter of the ongoing saga, for at the same time that humanity is bent on destructiveness, it is the bearer of divine beauty.

Having said what theological optimism is not, I now turn to a discussion of what theological optimism is. I begin with a definition: *theological optimism is a conviction that all of creation shares in the beauty of God.* The way in which humanity shares in the beauty of God specifically concerns the subject of the image of God. The declaration in Genesis 1 that every individual is made in the image of God was scandalous in the ancient world. The popular teaching was that only kings and pharaohs bore the image of one god or another. Coupled with this was the conviction that the chief end of humanity was to placate and satisfy the gods with offerings. Hebraic teaching challenged such conceptions in its declaration that every individual ("male and female") was made in the image of God.

The ethical implications of the image of God teaching have been tremendous. Being made in the image of God, every individual is of inestimable worth. This teaching says a loud No to every form of oppression—be it in political or social realms. Countless heroes of faith through the ages have decried despotism, bigotry, injustice, and greed that venerates wealth at the expense of people—for any slight against a human who bears the image of God is a slight against God. This was key to the efforts of William Wilberforce and the overturning of slavery, Florence Nightingale and nursing, Mahatma Gandhi and equality in the caste system, Tommy Douglas and universal health care, Martin Luther King Jr. and civil rights for African Americans, Desmond Tutu and apartheid in South Africa—and a host of other examples besides. Theological optimism is similarly positive with reference to the growth of the values of the kingdom in today's world. While human goodness may well be marred by sin, and while structural evil may abound, theological optimism declares that this is nevertheless God's world. Theological optimism celebrates all that is a natural outgrowth of the teachings of Jesus: universal health care and education, rights for children and for women, rights for the unborn and for minorities, rights for those with differing sexual orientations and for the worker, and rights for the mentally challenged and the physically handicapped. The theological optimist celebrates the ways in which the teaching of Jesus have transformed society—soup kitchens, food banks, clothing outlets, together with the many organizations that concern themselves with helping the deaf, the blind, the old, and the disabled.[5]

In my earlier discussions about faith and hope, I was compelled to introduce the subject of love. Doing so was necessary because both faith and hope find their fulfillment in love. It was with this in mind that the author of Colossians taught that "over all virtue put on love, which binds all virtues together in perfect unity" (Col 3:14). Just as the subjects of faith and hope overlap, so the subject of love overlaps with the subject of hope—for hope strives to actualize in the here and now the love that it anticipates in the there and then. Akin to how faith and hope seek to realize in this life what they know to be true in the next life, human love finds its fulfillment in divine love. It is for this reason that the Scriptures declare that "we love because he first loved us" (1 John 4:19). Human love finds its source in divine love. Doing good to and for others is certainly laudable, and something for which we should all strive; but doing good for others is only at its best when the motive for doing so stems from love for God. This distinction between "doing good" and "doing good in love" is present at the beginning of the love chapter.

> If I speak in the tongues of mortals and of angels, but do not have love, I am a noisy gong or a clanging cymbal. And if I have prophetic powers, and understand all

5. I anticipate the criticism that teaches that goodness in society is the product of humanism, not the teaching of Jesus. Such a criticism is circular, for it presupposes the very thing to which it objects—for humanism is itself a product of the teaching of Jesus: insofar as Jesus saw the inestimable worth of all people, and insofar as he emphasized love for one's enemies, turning the other cheek, the golden rule, forgiveness, and mercy, Jesus was the greatest humanist of all time. As such, secular humanism simply does not exist outside of a society that has not, at some level, embraced the humanitarian values of Jesus.

mysteries and all knowledge, and if I have all faith, so as to remove mountains, but do not have love, I am nothing. If I give away all my possessions, and if I hand over my body so that I may boast, but do not have love, I gain nothing. (1 Cor 13:1–3)

The distinction that Paul here drew between doing good and doing good in love is often overlooked. One may, like some of the Corinthians, have awe-inspiring charisms—such as the ability to speak in tongues or prophesy. One may be able to comprehend divine mysteries, and move mountains with great faith. One may give all that they possess to the poor, or die as a martyr—but all such actions only have merit before God if they are infused with love. Years ago I was challenged by the words of William Carey: "Expect great things for God; attempt great things from God." I have since concluded that the enormity of greatness is tied to the tininess of love. It is not, as Mother Theresa of Calcutta taught, great deeds that impress God, but little deeds with great love; and this is what followers of Jesus strive for—not first and foremost amazing accomplishments, but above all else a life that naturally infuses every action with love.

One challenge to growing in such love is the modern blight of individualism. A commonplace conviction is that if we are to love others, we must first love ourselves. In Christendom this conviction appears together with love for God and love for others. In order to buttress the conclusion that the Christian is mandated to love themselves, emphasis is placed on the fact that people bear the image of God, that God has forgiven them, that they are a child of the King, that they were saved from all eternity, and that God knew them before they were born. "If God loves me," it is queried, "who am I not to love myself?" When individualism is tied to entitlement, such convictions become yet more pronounced—"I deserve to be loved, for I am special," or "to mistreat me is to mistreat the anointed of God for I have been called and set apart." Such individualism is acutely present in worship music where the personal pronouns "I" and "me" abound, and where reference to the individual's emotional state predominate. Rarely, if ever, is it noted that such crass individualism appeared in Christian teaching precisely at the time that it appeared in the world. As with other examples, Christianity unwittingly sanctified and put a theological spin on Western society's concern with such matters as self-image, self-empowerment, and self-actualization. But Western society's fixation on the individual is contrary to faith. The Bible never enjoins the believer to love themselves. While there are many examples where the Bible exhorts the believer to love God and others, there is not a whisper in it that suggests that one should love oneself. The great commandment is no exception.

> Teacher, which commandment in the law is the greatest? Jesus said to him, "'You shall love the Lord your God with all your heart, and with all your soul, and with all your mind.' This is the greatest and first commandment. And a second is like it: 'You shall love your neighbour as yourself.' On these two commandments hang all the law and the prophets." (Matt 22:36–40)

It is contended by some that this passage makes a distinction between three loves: love for God, love for others, and love for self. But one must here be careful, for the "as yourself" of "you shall love your neighbour as yourself" is descriptive not prescriptive—it tells us how things are, not how things should be. The author of Ephesians suggests as much.

> In the same way, husbands should love their wives *as they do their own bodies*. He who loves his wife *loves himself*. For no one ever hates his own body, but he nourishes and tenderly cares for it, just as Christ does for the church, because we are members of his body. (Eph 5:28–30)

As with the great commandment, love for self in Ephesians is descriptive, not prescriptive. My contention that we are not called to love ourselves in no way endorses the opposite of self-love, for the pride that is present in self-love is equally present in self-loathing—the essential difference being that whereas self-love is narcissistic, self-loathing is masochistic. Nor does the fact that we are not called to love ourselves provide a license for the disciple to forego matters of self-care. Disciples might need to monitor their nutritional intake, their stress level, their sleep patterns, their leisure times, and their physical fitness—not at all because they deserve to do so, but simply because such self-care might better enable them to live in the kingdom.

As I noted in a previous chapter, the relationship between love for God and love for others collapses into one love. Given that "we love because God first loved us," the fact that love for people and love for God are one should occasion no surprise, for there is only one source of love. There are not two distinct types of love—a love for God and a different love for people. Because one's love for people is ultimately derived from love for God, the two loves are but different expressions of the one love. It is for this reason that the author of 1 John could state the following.

> Those who say, "I love God," and hate their brothers or sisters, are liars; for those who do not love a brother or sister whom they have seen, cannot love God whom they have not seen (1 John 4:20).

Love for Jesus leads to love for followers of Jesus: "Truly I tell you, just as you did it to one of the least of these who are members of my family, you did it to me" (Matt 25:40). Implicit to the teaching that the church is the "body of Christ" is the ontological solidarity that Jesus shares with those who are in him—such that any disregard expressed toward a disciple is disregard toward Jesus, even as love for a disciple is love for Jesus. Human love is on the same trajectory as love for God: insofar as one loves God, one will also love those who bear the image of God.

Bibliography

Barks, Coleman, ed. *The Essential Rumi*. San Francisco: HarperSanFrancisco, 1995.

"The Code of Hammurabi." *Internet Sacred Text Archive*. Evinity, 2011. http://www.sacred-texts.com/ane/ham/.

Pascal, Blaise. *Pensées*. Translation by A. J. Krailsheimer. New York: Penguin Classics, 1995.

Romero, Oscar A. *The Violence of Love*. Translation by James R. Brockman. Maryknoll, NY: Orbis, 2004

Thérèse of Lisieux. *The Story of a Soul*. London: Burns, Oates & Washbourne, 1922.